International Relations in
Europe, 1689–1789

IN THE SAME SERIES

General Editors: Eric J. Evans and P.D. King

LANCASTER PAMPHLETS

International Relations in Europe 1689–1789

J.H. Shennan

London and New York

First published 1995
by Routledge
11 Fetter Lane, London EC4P 4EE

Simultaneously published in the USA and Canada
by Routledge
29 West 35th Street, New York, NY 10001

© 1995 J.H. Shennan

Typeset in Bembo by
Ponting–Green Publishing Services, Chesham, Bucks
Printed and bound in Great Britain by
Clays Ltd, St Ives PLC

British Library Cataloguing in Publication Data
A catalogue record for this book is available from the British Library

Library of Congress Cataloging in Publication Data
Shennan, J. H.
International relations in Europe, 1689–1789/J.H. Shennan.
P.   cm. – (Lancaster pamphlets)
Includes bibliographical references.
1. Europe–Foreign relations.   I. Title.   II. Series.
D273.7.S44   1995
327.4–dc20   94–25627

ISBN 0–415–07780–X

Contents

Foreword

Lancaster Pamphlets offer concise and up-to-date accounts of major historical topics, primarily for the help of students preparing for Advanced Level examinations, though they should also be of value to those pursuing introductory courses in universities and other institutions of higher education. Without being all-embracing, their aims are to bring some of the central themes or problems confronting students and teachers into sharper focus than the textbook writer can hope to do; to provide the reader with some of the results of recent research which the textbook may not embody; and to stimulate thought about the whole interpretation of the topic under discussion.

Chronologies

Chronology of battles

1692	La Hogue	Anglo-Dutch victory in the Nine Years War (1688–97) ensuring command of the sea.
1700	Narva	Swedish victory in the Great Northern War (1700–21) on the Gulf of Finland over the Russian forces of Peter the Great.
1704	Blenheim	Victories over the French in the War of the Spanish Succession (1701–13) by the forces of the Grand Alliance, led by the Duke of Marlborough, the first (Blenheim) on the Danube, the remaining three in the Spanish Netherlands.
1706	Ramillies	
1708	Oudenarde	
1709	Malplaquet	
1707	Almanza	Franco-Spanish victory in Spain which secured the position of the Bourbon king, Philip V.
1709	Poltava	Crushing defeat of the Swedish army by Russia, marking the end of Swedish imperial ambitions.

1712	Denain	Significant French victory by Marshal Villars's army after the withdrawal of the English troops from the War of the Spanish Succession.
1714	Hangö	Russian naval victory over Sweden in the Great Northern War.
1718	Cape Passaro	British naval victory over Spain in the Mediterranean which forced Philip V to adhere to the Quadruple Alliance.
1734	Bitonto	Austrian defeat in Southern Italy by a combined Franco-Spanish army, a battle in the War of the Polish Succession (1733–38) which helped to fix the balance of power in the Peninsula for the rest of the century.
1741	Mollwitz	Prussian victory over the Austrian troops of Maria Theresa at the beginning of the War of the Austrian Succession (1740–48).
1742	Chotusitz	Victory by Frederick II of Prussia over Austrian forces which brought an end to the First Silesian War (1740–42).
1743	Dettingen	Victory near Frankfurt of an Anglo-Hanoverian army under the command of King George II over the French.
1745 (May)	Fontenoy	French victory under Marshal Saxe which reversed the defeat of Dettingen and gave France control of the Austrian Netherlands.
1745 (Sept.)	Bassignano	Defeat of Charles Emmanuel, Duke of Savoy, by Franco-Spanish forces in Italy during the War of the Austrian Succession.
1745 (June)	Hohenfriedberg	Decisive victories by Prussia in the Second Silesian War (1744–45) which ensured the incorporation of Silesia into Prussia.
1745 (Oct.)	Soor	

1746	Piacenza	Austro-Sardinian victory reversing the previous year's defeat at Bassingnano which confirmed the north–south Habsburg–Bourbon division of influence in Italy.
1757 (June)	Plassey	Decisive engagement near Calcutta between a British force led by Clive and a Nawabi army, which led to British control of Bengal.
1757 (July)	Hastenbeck	Defeat of the Duke of Cumberland by the French at the beginning of the Seven Years War (1756–63).
1757 (Nov.)	Rossbach	Victories by Frederick the Great, the first against French and imperial
1757 (Dec.)	Leuthen	troops, the second against an Austrian army of 90,000 men.
1758 (Aug.)	Zorndorf	Prussian victory over a Russian army besieging Custrine in Brandenburg.
1758 (Oct.)	Hochkirch	Defeat of Frederick the Great by the Austrians.
1759 (Aug.)	Kunersdorf	Austro-Russian victory over Frederick the Great.
1759 (Sept.)	Quebec	Decisive British victory in Canada over French forces.
1759 (Aug.)	Lagos	Decisive British naval victories against the French off Portugal and Brittany,
1759 (Nov.)	Quiberon Bay	depriving France of the ability to supply and reinforce her colonies.
1760	Torgau	Prussian victory against the Austrians which enabled Frederick the Great to seize control of Saxony.
1770	Chesmé	Overwhelming victory by the Russians over the Turkish fleet in the First Russo-Turkish War (1768–74).

| 1781 | Yorktown | British capitulation in Virginia to American and French forces, marking the effective end of the War of American Independence (1775–83). |

Chronology of treaties and alliances

1689	Grand Alliance of Vienna; the Emperor, Spain, England, the Dutch Republic, Savoy, Brandenburg–Prussia, Bavaria.
1697	Treaty of Ryswick, between the Emperor, England, Spain, the Dutch Republic and France, by which the Dutch Barrier was established, Louis XIV recognised William III as king of England and agreed to return Luxembourg to Spain and key fortresses on the right bank of the Rhine, including Philippsburg and Breisach, to the Empire.
1698	First Partition Treaty, between England, France and the Dutch Republic, which allocated most of Spain, the Spanish Netherlands, Sardinia and the overseas territories to the electoral prince of Bavaria, Joseph Ferdinand; Naples and Sicily, the Tuscan ports and the Basque province of Guipuzcoa to the Dauphin; and the duchy of Milan to the Emperor's younger son, Charles.
1699	Treaty of Carlowitz, between Austria, Poland, Venice and the Ottoman empire, by which the Turks ceded to the Austrian Habsburg empire Transylvania and Hungary (except for the Banat of Temesvar).
1700 (March)	Second Partition Treaty, between England, France and the Dutch Republic, adding Milan to the Dauphin's share of the Spanish empire as agreed in the first Partition Treaty, and naming Archduke Charles as heir to the territories previously apportioned to Joseph Ferdinand, the electoral prince of Bavaria.
1700 (June)	Treaty of Constantinople, between Muscovy and the Ottoman empire, by which Russia acquired Azov but failed to break through to the Black Sea.

1701	Grand Alliance of the Hague: England, the Dutch Republic and the Emperor, which called for a partition of the Spanish empire and the restoration of a Dutch barrier.
1713	Treaty of Utrecht, between Britain, the Dutch Republic, Prussia, Portugal, Savoy and France and Spain, by which Britain acquired Gibraltar and Minorca, Hudson's Bay, Newfoundland, Nova Scotia, Saint Kitts, and the right of *asiento*, and recognition of her Protestant succession; the Dutch regained their barrier.
1714 (March)	Treaty of Rastatt, between France and the Emperor, by which the Emperor acquired Milan, Naples, Sardinia and the former Spanish Netherlands, and Victor Amadeus, Duke of Savoy, became king of Sicily.
1714 (Sept.)	Treaty of Baden, between the Emperor (on behalf of the states of the Empire) and France, by which the electors of Bavaria and Cologne were reinstated, and France retained Strasbourg.
1715	Barrier Treaty, between Britain, the Emperor and the Dutch Republic.
1716	Treaty of Westminster, between Britain and the Emperor, by which Britain guaranteed the Emperor's possessions (excluding his claim to Spain), and the Emperor guaranteed the Hanoverian succession.
1717 (Jan.)	Triple Alliance of the Hague, between Britain, France and the Dutch Republic, whereby the Old Pretender was to be expelled from France, the fortifications at Dunkirk and Mardyk destroyed, and the British and French successions as established at Utrecht to be confirmed by the signatories.
1717 (Aug.)	Treaty of Amsterdam, between France, Russia and Prussia, whereby Russia and Prussia guaranteed the Utrecht settlement and France promised mediation to end the Northern War.
1718	Quadruple Alliance of London, between Britain, France, the Emperor and Savoy, by which the Emperor renounced his claim to the Spanish throne

and guaranteed the British and French successions as established at Utrecht; Sardinia was handed over to the Duke of Savoy in exchange for Sicily, which went to the Emperor; and the children of Philip V of Spain and Elizabeth Farnese became heirs to Parma and Tuscany.

1719 (Jan.)	Treaty of Vienna, between Hanover, the Emperor and Saxony/Poland, which aimed at forcing Tsar Peter I to evacuate Mecklenburg and Poland.
1719 (Nov.)	Treaty of Stockholm, between Sweden and Hanover, by which Hanover acquired Bremen and Verden.
1720 (Feb.)	Treaty of Stockholm, between Sweden and Prussia, by which Prussia acquired most of western Pomerania.
1720 (June)	Treaty of Fredericksburg, between Sweden and Denmark, by which Denmark acquired Schleswig.
1721 (June)	Triple Alliance of Madrid, between France, Spain and Britain, renewing the mutual guarantees relating to the British and French successions as established at Utrecht and to Parma and Tuscany as agreed in the Quadruple Alliance of London.
1721 (Sept.)	Treaty of Nystad, between Sweden and Russia, by which Russia acquired Livonia, Estonia, Ingria and parts of Karelia.
1725 (April)	(First) Treaty of Vienna, between the Emperor and Spain, by which the Emperor confirmed the succession to Parma and Tuscany of Philip V's two sons, and Spain guaranteed the Pragmatic Sanction and conferred trading rights upon the Ostend Company.
1725 (Sept.)	Treaty of Hanover, between Britain, France and Prussia, by which the three signatories guaranteed each other's territories inside and outside Europe.
1726	Russia joins the first Treaty of Vienna of 1725.
1727	Preliminaries of Paris, signed by Britain, France, the United Provinces and the Emperor, which reaffirmed the terms of the Quadruple Alliance and suspended the Ostend Company's trading.

1728	Convention of the Pardo. Spain adds her signature to the Preliminaries of Paris.
1731	(Second) Treaty of Vienna, between Britain and Austria, by which each guaranteed the possessions of the other, the Emperor agreed to suppress the Ostend Company and to allow Philip V's son, Don Carlos, to enter Italy as Duke of Parma. Spain and the Dutch Republic both adhered to this treaty and, with Britain, guaranteed the Pragmatic Sanction.
1733 (Sept.)	Treaty of Turin, between France and Savoy/ Sardinia, by which France promised to support the duke of Savoy's efforts to gain the Milanese from the Emperor.
1733 (Nov.)	Treaty of the Escorial (first Family Compact), between France and Spain, by which the two Bourbon powers guaranteed each other's territories in Europe and overseas, and sought to destroy the Emperor's power in the Italian peninsula.
1738	(Third) Treaty of Vienna, between France and Austria, by which France finally guaranteed the Pragmatic Sanction in return for the reversion of Lorraine; Don Carlos became king of the Two Sicilies; the Duke of Savoy acquired part of the Milanese and the Emperor acquired Parma and Piacenza. In addition, the former duke of Lorraine inherited Tuscany, and Augustus III was confirmed as king of Poland.
1739	Treaty of Belgrade, between Russia, Austria and the Ottoman empire, whereby French mediation restored Turkish security around the Black Sea and French influence in Constantinople.
1741 (June)	First Treaty of Breslau, between France and Prussia, providing French support for Prussia's seizure of Silesia.
1741 (Oct.)	Convention of Kleinschnellendorf, between Prussia and Austria, by which Prussia withdrew temporarily from the First Silesian War.
1742	Second Treaty of Breslau, between Prussia and Austria, ending the First Silesian War and leaving Prussia in possession of Silesia.

1743	Treaty of Fontainebleau (second Family Compact), between France and Spain, committing France to support Spain's territorial ambitions in the Italian peninsula.
1745	Treaty of Dresden, between Prussia and Austria, ending the Second Silesian War and confirming Prussia's acquisition of Silesia.
1746	Two Empresses Treaty of St Petersburg, between Austria and Russia, a defensive alliance aimed against Prussia.
1748	Treaty of Aix-la-Chapelle, between France, Britain, the Dutch Republic, Austria, Spain and Sardinia, largely restoring the status quo at the end of the War of the Austrian Succession.
1752	Treaty of Aranjuez, between Austria, Sardinia and Spain, by which the signatories guaranteed each other's Italian possessions.
1755	Convention of St Petersburg, between Britain and Russia, by which Britain subsidised the costs of a Russian army as a means of securing Hanover from attack.
1756 (Jan.)	Convention of Westminster, between Britain and Prussia, guaranteeing the neutrality of the German states.
1756 (May)	First Treaty of Versailles, a defensive alliance between France and Austria, joined by Russia in December.
1757 (May)	Second Treaty of Versailles, an offensive alliance between France and Austria.
1757 (Sept.)	Convention of Kloster-Zeven, between Britain and France, leaving Hanover under French control.
1761	Third Family Compact, between France and Spain, guaranteeing mutual support in the colonial struggle against Britain.
1763 (Feb.)	Treaty of Hubertusburg, between Austria, Prussia and Saxony/Poland, confirming Prussia's possession of Silesia.

1763 (Feb.)	Treaty of Paris, between France, Britain and Spain, by which Britain made extensive gains from France and Spain, in North America, the West Indies, India, Africa and Europe.
1764	Russo-Prussian defensive alliance, allowing Catherine II to intervene in Poland and securing Frederick II against Austrian attempts to regain Silesia.
1772	First Partition of Poland (Conventions of St Petersburg), between Russia, Prussia and Austria, allocating Livonia and White Russia to Russia, Galicia to Austria and Polish Prussia to Prussia.
1774	Treaty of Kuchuk-Kainardji, between Russia and the Ottoman empire, by which Russia reached the north shore of the Black Sea and the Turks recognised Russia's right to intercede on behalf of the Porte's Orthodox Christian subjects.
1779	Treaty of Teschen, between Austria and Prussia, ending the War of the Bavarian Succession.
1780	The Armed Neutrality between Russia, the Dutch Republic, Austria, Prussia, Portugal, Sweden and Norway, established to protect the rights of neutral trade at sea.
1783	Treaty of Versailles, between France, Spain, the Dutch Republic and Britain, ending the War of American Independence and depriving Britain of her American colonies, of Florida and Minorca which were restored to Spain, and of Tobago in the West Indies and the Senegal river in West Africa which were returned to France.

1

Introduction

By the end of the seventeenth century international relations were becoming more complex as the criteria by which they operated underwent subtle change. In considering how seventeenth-century governments acted *vis-à-vis* their neighbours we must first recognise that almost all the significant countries in Europe – the Dutch Republic was the great exception – were ruled by kings and princes. That fact explains the assumptions underlying many issues of foreign policy. Kings governed according to dynastic precepts, of which the most important was the law of succession.

Louis XIV, for example, inherited the crown of France as head of the Bourbon family and his right of inheritance was according to rules analogous to those governing the contractual relationships between private individuals. Consequently he was inclined to assert and protect his rights against the rest of Europe in rather the same way as a wealthy subject might have recourse to the law in support of his claims against a neighbour. It was a matter of family honour. The famous concept of *gloire*, in which Louis took such pride, was less about military prowess than about defending the family's reputation in the eyes of contemporaries and of posterity. Indeed, because many of the ruling dynasties of Europe were interrelated, diplomatic and military conflicts often had the appearance of family quarrels. Louis XIV's mother, Anne of Austria, was a Spanish princess

1

(her title a reminder of the close family links between Spanish and Austrian Habsburgs), and Louis himself was the great-grandson of Philip II of Spain.

That is why one of the abiding interests of Louis XIV's life was the question of who should inherit the Spanish empire after the death of the last Spanish Habsburg, the childless Charles II (1661–1700). His great rival in the pursuit of that rich inheritance was the Habsburg Holy Roman Emperor, Leopold I (1640–1705). Leopold's mother, Maria Anna (d.1646), was the younger daughter of King Philip III of Spain (1578–1621) whereas Anne of Austria (d.1666), Louis XIV's mother, was the elder daughter. To complete the symmetrical pattern of these Bourbon–Habsburg family relationships, Leopold's first wife, Margaret (d.1673), was the younger daughter of King Philip IV of Spain (1605–65) while Louis's wife, Maria Teresa (d.1683), was the elder. It is little wonder that the question of who was to succeed Charles II began increasingly to preoccupy rulers and their advisers as the seventeenth century drew towards its close.

In fact the problem of the Spanish succession provides one of the keys to an understanding of how the character of international relations changed and developed over the whole of this period. The Spanish succession raised questions about the English, and the Scottish and Irish, successions and also about the succession in France. The rhetoric of eighteenth-century war and diplomacy in Europe – the wars of the Polish, Austrian and Bavarian successions – continued to emphasise that pre-eminently dynastic and personalised aspect of international relations. However, the rhetoric increasingly failed to match the reality. Fundamental policy objectives began to alter as dynastic considerations were challenged by requirements of national and international security, and sometimes by the wider interests of subjects. In the course of this shift the relationships between European states, north, south, east and west, became less regionally discreet and more interdependent.

The rivalry between the two great dynastic houses of Habsburg and Bourbon provided one of the two chief stimuli for the regulation of international relationships in the later years of the seventeenth century as it had done for several generations previously. The second source of friction, as yet subordinate but potentially of great significance, was European expansion overseas. In this sphere too Habsburg and Bourbon rivalry was prominent but there were other equally important players, notably the English and the Dutch. Although the latter's United Provinces only formally acquired their sovereignty at the Peace of Westphalia (1648) they had enjoyed effective independence since the earlier successful revolt against Philip II's Spain. Overseas rivalries had a subtly different character from those based on traditional territorial disputes in Europe which, as we have seen, were pursued in the interests of ruling princes and in the language of their legally inherited rights.

The prominent role of the United Provinces of the Dutch Republic in extra-European affairs is significant in this regard. For the Dutch had acquired their independence by rejecting princely power altogether and establishing a republican form of government. Inevitably, therefore, their external interests and their motivation reflected a different set of values from those of their former rulers. The Dutch East India Company, for example, was a joint-stock enterprise, established in 1602 for the benefit of its shareholders, mainly the wealthy burghers of Amsterdam. It acquired considerable political authority in the overseas regions under its domination (notably the Indonesian archipelago, parts of India and Ceylon), including the right to declare war or make peace, to establish colonies and to coin money. The dominant political families in Holland who controlled central government policy were also the chief beneficiaries of the commercial riches netted from the Indies, although all Dutchmen were eligible as investors. The pursuit of economic prosperity became the supreme objective of state policy, though the Dutch failed to come to terms with the critical fact that wealth on its own account did not provide security; that had still to be purchased. Later events would suggest that the political culture of the United Provinces could not reconcile the uninhibited pursuit of wealth with the maintenance of national security.

This dilemma was also faced by England which had similarly invested heavily in overseas colonies. The political structures of the two countries had much in common, particularly during the period of the Commonwealth (1649–60) and later, from 1689, when the Dutch stadholder William of Orange (1689–1702) ascended the English throne. English joint-stock companies were established to trade with the colonies and an increasingly powerful trading lobby found its voice in the House of Commons. However, the English government regulated economic policy

3

without endangering national security. Its various Navigation Acts (1651, 1660, 1669) were declarations of economic warfare against any rival seeking to profit from England's colonial wealth. That wealth was to be safeguarded not only by statute but also by the burgeoning power of the royal navy.

The importance of this extra-European dimension in seventeenth-century international relations should not be exaggerated. The main focus of concern remained within Europe. Yet it is surely the case that European rivalries played out beyond the continent must at some stage modify traditional diplomatic attitudes. In particular the central problem of colonial expansion, how to procure additional wealth from trade without risking the nation's security, inevitably weakened the dominant theme of dynasticism.

PART I

Succession crises

2

The English succession

Over a decade before the issue of the Spanish succession came to a head Europe's rulers had to come to terms with another succession, in England in 1689. James II, head of the hereditary ruling house of Stuart, was replaced by his elder daughter Mary (1689–94) and, more significantly, by her husband William, Duke of Orange and stadholder of the Dutch Republic. This so-called 'Glorious Revolution' brought into the same camp the two leading Protestant maritime powers of western Europe. Their alliance under William's leadership ended a generation of economic rivalry and warfare and signalled the beginning of a policy of common cause against the threat of French expansionism under Louis XIV. The counter-threat from London and the Hague was a serious one. For William's accession to the English throne challenged the principle of dynastic inheritance everywhere. Despite the attendant plethora of legal and constitutional arguments there was no disguising the central fact that the king of England by right of inheritance had been forced to leave his throne; and the succession had been skewed in order to eliminate his young heir, the future Old Pretender. The Declaration of Rights was the work of the two houses of lords and commons, so it could be argued that the English political nation had asserted the supremacy of its interests over those of royal dynasticism, a factor of considerable importance in the future conduct of English foreign policy.

Shortly before the 'Glorious Revolution' Louis XIV had again embarked upon an aggressive policy on his eastern frontier. For over a century French kings had viewed this Rhineland region as part of the front line of their defences against the Habsburgs. In the autumn of 1688 French troops occupied the bishopric of Cologne and invested the fortress of Phillipsburg in the Palatinate. Louis justified his actions in part on familiar dynastic grounds: his sister-in-law was also the sister of the late Elector Palatine and could make some claim to the succession. But behind this conventional justification lurked the fear that without a pre-emptive strike Louis's most vulnerable frontier would be exposed to attack from his arch-rival, the Habsburg Emperor Leopold I. For some time the Emperor had been preoccupied with the problems on his eastern frontier. However, the Turkish siege of Vienna had been relieved in 1683 and since then Leopold had made great strides towards stabilising the region, beginning the process of incorporating under his direct rule the large province of Transylvania. He was therefore ready to turn his attention westwards where the great prize of the Spanish succession beckoned.

What most dramatically altered the balance of forces at this juncture, however, was the capture of the English throne by William of Orange in November 1688. The effect of that *coup* was to deprive Louis of a reliable if somewhat unwilling ally in the Stuart king James II and to bring into being a formidable anti-French coalition. The League of Augsburg (1686), consisting of the Emperor, Spain, Sweden and a number of German princes, was the basis of a new coalition, the Grand Alliance of Vienna (May 1689), whose signatories eventually included the Emperor, Spain, England, the Dutch Republic, Savoy and, among the leading German principalities, Brandenburg–Prussia and Bavaria. The Nine Years War (1688–97) saw Louis fighting in isolation against a formidable alliance intent upon reducing French frontiers to less threatening limits. The war ended in 1697 with the Treaty of Ryswick. The territorial settlement reflected the evenly matched powers of the combatants. On his vulnerable eastern flank Louis was forced to cede the fortress of Luxembourg and withdraw his troops from Lorraine; but he held on to earlier gains in Alsace (including Strasbourg), the three bishoprics of Metz, Toul and Verdun, and Franche-Comté. He did, however, agree to recognise William III as *de facto* king of England, and to permit the establishment of a defensive line of barrier fortresses, manned by the Dutch, on the border between France and the Spanish Netherlands.

Despite continuing to shelter the exiled James II whose *de jure* claims to the English and Scottish crowns he continued to support, Louis was forced to recognise the political reality of William's position. It was a disagreeable posture for such a staunch advocate of divine-right, dynastic kingship to have to adopt, but at least he had only succumbed after fighting a long war. The Emperor, every bit as zealous a dynast as Louis, had fought the war as William's ally. In his case too necessity triumphed over principle. Leopold's eyes were firmly fixed on the Spanish succession and upon the ailing figure of the childless King of Spain, Charles II. In the Grand Alliance of Vienna William had promised his support to the Habsburg camp.

The attitudes displayed by Louis XIV and Leopold I raise the daunting question of the place of morality in international affairs. In discussing this subject the danger is always to assume that political decisions are comparable with personal credos of right and wrong. That danger exists precisely because political decisions have always been – and continue to be – interpreted through a moral vocabulary. This happens because any other justification would appear anti-social. Yet even the dynastic rulers of the seventeenth century, who believed strongly in the legal assertion of their inherited family rights, were not in precisely the same position as their more litigious subjects. For the prince's first obligation was to provide security for his subjects; without it their loyalty could be neither guaranteed nor expected. The prince would invariably seek to base his territorial claims upon sound legal foundations, otherwise his own reputation and the honour of his family would be damaged. Sometimes, however, the need to ensure the integrity of his state forced him to take actions without any satisfactory legal justification. That tendency was destined to grow with the development of the early modern European state system. By the late seventeenth century the scale and complexity of government action had greatly increased, driven by the need to support ever larger armies and navies. In addition, the principle of *cuius regio eius religio* adopted during the sixteenth-century religious wars, which required all the subjects to adopt their ruler's religion, had had the effect of uniting government and governed, though

9

not in the furtherance of confessional causes. For although appeals to religious solidarity remained part of the rhetoric of politics, the greater union thus established between government and people led paradoxically towards the concept of the state as a secular entity. Two further related developments followed. First, 'great-power' Europe began to emerge, potentially a most dangerous and unstable world, though one increasingly aware of the need for rules of international behaviour. Hugo Grotius, the father of international law, sought to fill that vacuum in 1625 with the publication of *De jure belli ac pacis*. Secondly, the idea began dimly to take shape that the prince's personal interests would have to be reconciled with those of the national community, however defined. Thus by 1697, at the Treaty of Ryswick, the international community was already prepared to recognise as king of England not God's nominee but parliament's, and by allowing the Dutch to garrison certain fortresses bordering the Spanish Netherlands and France – the famous barrier – to recognise the concept of national security.

3

The Spanish succession

The partition treaties

One reason for Louis XIV's willingness to make peace at Ryswick on relatively unfavourable terms was his fear that the King of Spain might die before hostilities ceased, thereby weakening Louis's hopes of enforcing his family's claim against that of his Habsburg rival. In 1698 Louis approached William III to suggest that in order to ensure the future peace and security of Europe the two monarchs, in collaboration with the Dutch, should agree a partition of the Spanish empire, to take effect after the death of Charles II. The idea of partition was not new: in 1668 Louis and Emperor Leopold had signed a partition treaty based upon their mutual recognition, despite the refusal of each to yield to the other over the merits of his claim, of the need for compromise in order to avoid the alternative of prolonged upheaval in Europe. This agreement, subsequently rejected as void by both parties, reflects the long-established preference among rulers and diplomats for a balance of power which would contribute to stability. What Louis XIV and William III were attempting to achieve in 1698 and 1700, when the two partition treaties were signed, was something much more revolutionary. For William III had no claim whatever to the Spanish inheritance. He was, however, the most powerful ruler in western Europe apart from Louis himself; the hope of

11

the two rulers, therefore, was that together they might enforce a settlement, and thereby preserve Europe from renewed warfare. This was the beginning of the idea of collective security whereby the great powers would seek to impose solutions upon European, later world, problems. The vastness of the Spanish empire made Louis realise that the traditional rules of dynastic inheritance could not be applied with any expectation of success. Rather, they would provide the justification for claimants to acquire a share.

There were three such claimants: the Emperor himself; Louis XIV's son, the Dauphin, through his mother Maria Teresa; and the infant electoral prince of Bavaria, Joseph Ferdinand, through his mother, who was a daughter of the Emperor. The First Partition Treaty, that of 1698, allocated the bulk of the empire – most of Spain itself, the Spanish Netherlands, Sardinia and the overseas territories – to the least threatening candidate, Joseph Ferdinand; the duchy of Milan to the Emperor's younger son, Archduke Charles; and Naples and Sicily, the Tuscan ports and the Basque province of Guipuzcoa to the Dauphin. Additional clauses invited other European states to adhere to the treaty and to commit themselves, with the three original signatories, England, France and the Dutch Republic, to enforcing the settlement contained therein. In this regard the treaty bore some resemblance to contemporary United Nations resolutions.

This was indeed a revolutionary change in the conduct of international affairs and it is not surprising that in the course of negotiations one of the main protagonists, Louis XIV, should have vacillated between old principles and new. He was convinced of the pre-eminence of the laws of hereditary succession, as he was to demonstrate provocatively in 1701 by recognising the Old Pretender as King James III. Yet he was also willing to contemplate the elector of Bavaria's succession to his son's portion of the Spanish inheritance if the electoral prince were to die without heirs. This was despite the fact that Joseph Ferdinand's claim came exclusively through Maria Antonia, his mother. More striking still was Louis's willingness, not finally reflected in the treaty itself, to contemplate ceding parts of the Spanish empire in the Mediterranean to William in order to safeguard English and Dutch trade.

The death in 1699 of Joseph Ferdinand, the electoral prince of Bavaria, necessitated the drawing up of the Second Partition

Treaty (1700), again signed by England, France and the Dutch Republic. The Spanish empire was now to be divided between the surviving two candidates. Archduke Charles was to receive most of Spain, the Spanish Netherlands, Sardinia and the overseas empire, while the Dauphin would acquire Milan to add to the other Italian and Spanish possessions named in the first treaty. The principle of collective security with its underlying threat of force was carried a stage further in this treaty. Milan was to be exchanged for Lorraine, thereby firmly locking France's vulnerable eastern frontier and leaving the unfortunate Duke of Lorraine to establish a new patrimony in northern Italy. William and Louis also discussed the possibility, halted by the death of the King of Spain, of a further exchange, Savoy for Naples and Sicily. These proposed exchanges indicate clearly the extent to which security needs overcame all other considerations. That factor also accounts for the clause in the treaty which stipulated that the portion of the Spanish inheritance allotted to the Archduke could never be united to the Austrian domains.

However, the primacy of security still required justification. In the period before and during the War of the Spanish Succession the significance of the national interest in providing that justification was sometimes dimly perceived, either as a positive force or as an obstacle to be reckoned with. The revolution of 1688 had proclaimed the national interest of the English, but this had been at the expense of the Scots and Irish who remained loyal to the house of Stuart. During the War of the Spanish Succession the Castilians were to remain loyal to the new King of Spain, Louis XIV's grandson, Philip V. Indeed, without their commitment Spain would have been lost to the Bourbons. In the darkest days of the war Louis himself was to come close to appealing for the support of the French nation in order to continue the struggle against the Grand Alliance, going so far as to issue a letter to his provincial governors which justified a renewed war effort in the light of the enemy's unacceptable demands.

Charles II of Spain died in November 1700. His last will and testament bequeathed the entire Spanish empire to Louis XIV's second grandson, Philip of Anjou. When the Spanish emissaries bearing the news reached Versailles, Louis was faced with a dilemma which he himself recognised as intractable. If he

13

rejected the terms of the will – and he always maintained that his grandson's rights were by birth and not through the will – the same offer would be made in Vienna in favour of the archduke Charles. For what the Spaniards wanted above all was to avoid the partition of their empire. Louis was also well aware of the fact that the emperor, Leopold, had no intention of recognising the partition treaties. That being so, it would have been naive of the French king to assume that the Emperor's allies against Louis in the Nine Years War, the Dutch and the English, would take up arms against Leopold, and against Spain, to enforce the terms of the second Partition Treaty. After some days of solemn reflection Louis signalled to the world that he had recognised his grandson as Philip V of Spain.

The War of the Spanish Succession

There is little point in seeking to attribute blame for the war which followed. Provocations were readily identified. In 1701 Leopold's forces invaded Milan, and in the same year French troops seized the Dutch barrier fortresses and Louis recognised the Old Pretender as King James III. However, the American historian, William Roosen, has shrewdly observed that war was probably unavoidable from the moment of Joseph Ferdinand's death, for the electoral prince of Bavaria was the only candidate for the succession who could have maintained the unity of the Spanish empire without threatening the balance of power.[1] Once that alternative was removed the great powers had only their conflicting interests and mutual suspicions to fall back on, and in that situation war was the likely outcome.

Once begun, the War of the Spanish Succession followed an unpredictable course. That is true of all wars but in this case the unpredictability was exacerbated by the widely different interests and motives of the chief belligerents. For England the primary war aim was to guarantee the Protestant succession by forcing Louis XIV to recognise Queen Anne and her successors (the Protestant daughter of James II having succeeded William III in 1702). The Emperor, already embarrassed by the necessity of having himself to recognise the Protestant succession, was far more concerned with the fate of the Spanish empire's Italian possessions, notably Milan. That duchy was the crucial corridor

14

linking the Spanish and Austrian Habsburg lands. Were it to fall into French hands, not only would that link be broken but the hereditary lands of the Austrian Habsburgs would be vulnerable to attack. The Dutch, on the other hand, were more concerned with the security of their own southern frontier and with the future political organisation of the Spanish Netherlands. Louis XIV, who was himself accused of aspiring to universal monarchy, was conscious of the threat to the balance of power posed by recent Habsburg successes against the Turks in eastern Europe. That was not the perception of the Maritime Powers, the Dutch and the English, who were preoccupied with the security of western and southern Europe, and with the trading opportunities thereby guaranteed. In 1703 the English Whig ministry was largely responsible for a further extension of the war aims to include the securing of the whole of the Spanish empire for the archduke Charles. (Before the war was declared in 1701 both Maritime Powers had recognised Philip of Anjou's accession as Philip V.) This policy was not much favoured by the Dutch, nor even by the Emperor, who feared that in the struggle for Spain his Italian interests might be sacrificed in some subsequent partition of the Spanish empire. In addition, from 1703 Leopold was faced with a full-scale rebellion in Hungary which for most of the war limited the extent of his commitment in the west.

One result of the decision by the Grand Alliance of the Hague to support Archduke Charles's candidature to succeed in Spain and the Indies was to rekindle the ancient rivalry between Castile and Catalonia. The Catalans supported the Archduke and that was sufficient to persuade Castile to remain loyal to Philip V. So effective was that support that in mainland Spain the Grand Alliance came off second best, in sharp contrast to its successes in the Low Countries, Italy, Germany, the Mediterranean and the overseas world. The seeds of the ultimate compromise reached at the Peace of Utrecht grew out of that failure. So great were the suspicions among the allies of Louis XIV's ambitions that they were inclined to demand something approaching unconditional surrender before bringing hostilities to an end. In 1709, therefore, when Louis's fortunes were at their lowest ebb, they made of him perhaps the only demand that he felt unable to countenance. This was the requirement that if necessary the King himself should make war upon his

15

grandson to force him out of Spain. After these notorious Preliminaries of 1709 had been rejected, French fortunes improved. In 1710 a new Tory ministry in England dropped the 'no peace without Spain' demand which had been at the heart of the Whigs' war effort. In 1711 upon the death of his elder brother, Emperor Joseph I, Archduke Charles became Emperor Charles VI, and the threat of a new Habsburg Empire to rival that of Charles V in the sixteenth century rapidly reduced the level of his support from the English and Dutch governments. With the withdrawal of the formidable Duke of Marlborough from the fray as a result of the infamous 'restraining orders' issued by the new Tory government, the French armies were able to regain something of their former reputation. Marshal Villars's victory at Denain (1712) boosted French morale, though it could not offset the impressive litany of allied victories at Blenheim (1704), Ramillies (1706), Oudenarde (1708) and Malplaquet (1709).

The Peace of Utrecht

The Peace of Utrecht consisted of the treaties of Utrecht (1713), Rastatt and Baden (1714). The terms were essentially agreed between Britain and France and represented the sort of compromise which had seemed unlikely in 1709–10. The Spanish empire was, finally, partitioned. Philip V remained King of Spain and the Indies. In the Mediterranean, Gibraltar and Minorca went to Britain; in Italy, Milan, Naples and Sardinia went to Emperor Charles VI, the former Archduke Charles, who also acquired the Spanish (henceforth the Austrian) Netherlands. In return for his support of the Grand Alliance Victor Amadeus of Savoy was made King of Sicily. The Dutch barrier of fortresses in the southern Netherlands was revived. Overseas, Britain gained Hudson's Bay, Newfoundland, Nova Scotia and the West Indian island of Saint Kitts from France, and the right of *asiento*, permission to import African slaves to the Spanish colonies, from Spain. France also lost Tournai on her vulnerable north-eastern frontier to the Dutch barrier, but retained Lille, Condé and Maubeuge, as well as the key city of Strasbourg in Alsace, all of which Louis had been resigned to losing in 1709. Finally, France guaranteed the Protestant succession to the

British throne (England and Scotland having been declared a unitary state by the Act of Union of 1707), and Philip V renounced his claim to succeed to the throne of France.

In guaranteeing the successions in Britain and France the Peace of Utrecht marked an important stage in the development of the idea of collective security. In order to anticipate and prevent conflicts likely to arise from the application of old dynastic principles, the powers sought to impose a new international order justified solely by the need to prevent war. There was a particular irony in the juxtaposition of these two guarantees, as Mark A. Thomson has pointed out: 'it is surely strange that the very treaties that forced England's enemies to acknowledge the right of the British to choose their own form of government should have denied that right to France'.[2] Neither Louis XIV nor his grandson believed that Philip V's renunciation would stand if the young child destined to become Louis XV should die without heirs. The vexed question of the two successions, now permanently intertwined as a result of the peace, would remain an issue for some time to come.

In territorial terms Utrecht represented something of a compromise. Among the great powers France, the Emperor and Spain could all draw some satisfaction from the settlement, though none had achieved all their aims. Paradoxically, it was Britain, with no claim to the Spanish Succession, which made potentially important gains, in the Mediterranean, the West Indies and North America. However, the real significance of these acquisitions was that they reflected the British desire for a trading hegemony backed by a permanent navy, which by the end of the War of the Spanish Succession dominated the seas. In contrast the Dutch, exhausted by decades of war against France, had become the junior partner of the Maritime Powers, inclined to follow where Britain led.

As with all major peace settlements Utrecht failed to restore unalloyed tranquillity. The uncertainties surrounding the British and French successions remained potentially dangerous. Charles VI and Philip V had signed no agreement. The former refused to recognise the latter as king of Spain or the settlement in Italy as definitive. For his part Philip V still hoped to recover some of the Italian lands which had formerly belonged to the Spanish empire. Many opportunities remained for the renewal of serious international rivalry. Finally, the Great Northern War (1700–21) was still being waged, and although that conflict had scarcely impinged upon the War of the Spanish Succession it would increasingly concern the wider international community after Utrecht.

4

The Baltic succession

Swedish imperialism

At the Peace of Westphalia (1648) Sweden emerged as the dominant power in the Baltic region. She acquired Bremen, Verden and Wismar in the Holy Roman Empire, and western Pomerania on the southern shore of the Baltic. These, and earlier territorial additions giving Sweden control of Finland, Ingria, Estonia and Livonia, threatened to transform the Baltic into a Swedish lake. Indeed, the thrust of Swedish policy ever since the establishment of the Vasa dynasty (1525) had been to create a Baltic empire. The newly independent state of Sweden had few natural resources and only a small population. The region's greatest wealth lay in the lucrative Baltic trade which the Swedes aspired to take over. If they were to succeed in that ambition they would have to control the important Baltic ports and the river mouths opening into the Baltic sea. However, the gradual encirclement of the Baltic littoral in pursuit of that aim stretched Sweden's resources to the limit. Each additional commitment added to her vulnerability as much as to her strength. The power of the Swedish empire therefore rested upon a fragile foundation, particularly since after Westphalia her arch-enemy Denmark still possessed Scania, on the southern tip of the Swedish peninsula, and therefore maintained control of the access to the Baltic through the Sound channel. For some years after 1648 Sweden maintained her expansionist policy. Charles X (1654–60) declared war on Poland in 1655 (the War of the North) in the hope of acquiring the port of Danzig. He failed in this aim but succeeded in wresting Scania from the Danes by the Treaty of Copenhagen (1660).

One effect of Swedish imperialism was to cause unease among the Maritime Powers. The Dutch in particular had a large stake in the grain trade through Danzig, and both the Dutch and the English depended upon Baltic naval stores for the maintenance of their fleets. During Charles X's campaign the Dutch Republic used its diplomatic endeavours to prevent Sweden from adding to its domination of the region, especially by the capture of Danzig. The War of the North was concluded through the diplomatic good offices of France. Sweden had been a French ally since the days of King Gustavus Adolphus's involvement in the Thirty Years War (1618–48) and the French were keen to maintain a relationship which would help to offset Habsburg power in Germany.

Charles XI (1660–97) profited from this relationship at the end of the Scanian War (1676–79) against Denmark. Despite suffering a series of defeats the Swedes were able to preserve the status quo in the Treaty of Lund, thanks to the powerful intervention of Louis XIV. However, Charles XI was on the point of undertaking a dramatic reversal of Swedish policy, forsaking the traditional aggressive expansionism of his predecessors in favour of neutrality. The Swedish army, for so long considered invincible in the north, had been defeated in 1675 at the Battle of Fehrbellin by the rising power of Brandenburg–Prussia. The Elector of Brandenburg, 'the Great Elector', having already acquired eastern Pomerania on the Baltic at the Peace of Westphalia, was casting envious eyes at the adjacent Swedish Pomerania. Further east, the ancient struggle between Poland–Lithuania and Muscovy was at last beginning to turn in the latter's favour. At the Peace of Andrusovo (1667) the Muscovites regained the key cities of Kiev and Smolensk on the river Dnieper. This signal victory opened the way for renewed Russian contacts with the west and turned Moscow's attention once more to the Baltic. On several previous occasions the Muscovites had succeeded briefly in breaking through to the Baltic shore. Their most recent attempt had ended in 1617 when, at the Treaty of Stolbova, the Swedes acquired Ingria at

20

the eastern end of the Gulf of Finland and once more excluded Muscovy from the Baltic. Charles XI appreciated that new predators were now joining the old enemy Denmark in seeking to dismember Sweden's vulnerable empire. He knew too that the Swedish navy could no longer dominate the Baltic. Power there lay with the Dutch and English fleets which were determined to prevent any state in the region from threatening their trading interests. Against this background Charles XI chose a policy of neutrality which protected Sweden and the whole Baltic region from involvement in the Nine Years War. Charles XI died in 1697, the year in which Muscovy's ambitious young tsar Peter I (1682–1725) embarked upon his 'Great Embassy' to western Europe.

The Great Northern War

Peter's original intention in visiting the west had been to explore the possibility of recruiting a powerful alliance against the Ottoman empire. In 1696 his forces had captured Azov in a thrust towards the northern shores of the Black Sea, and he was convinced that Turkish power was now vulnerable in the region. He discovered, however, that in western Europe it was the issue of the Spanish succession that was attracting the attention of rulers and diplomats. That applied in particular to Peter's chief ally in the region, the Austrian Habsburg Emperor Leopold. In fact the Austrians made peace with the Turks at Carlowitz in 1699, seeking at the same time to persuade Peter to continue the war in order to protect their south-eastern frontiers. Peter was forced therefore to reconsider the direction of his foreign policy. His desire for a foothold on the Baltic predated his journey to the west and that ambition grew with the lack of international support for his anti-Turkish crusade. He was encouraged by the succession to the Swedish throne in 1697 of an inexperienced fifteen year-old king, Charles XII (1697–1718), and by the election in the same year of Frederick Augustus, Elector of Saxony, as King of Poland (1697–1706). The latter was keen to restore Poland's flagging reputation as an international force in northern and eastern Europe by attempting to regain Livonia from Sweden, together with its important port of Riga. Once he had signed the Treaty of Constantinople in 1700, ending the war

21

against the Ottoman empire, Peter was ready with his new allies, Poland and Denmark, to attack Charles XII of Sweden.

The key events of the first part of the war can be elaborated briefly. Not for the last time in his reign Peter underestimated both the strength of the opposition and the weakness of his allies. The Danes were immediately overwhelmed by Swedish troops and sued for peace, and the Polish invasion of Livonia likewise ended in a humiliating withdrawal. Peter laid siege to Narva, the scene of Ivan the Terrible's assault on the Baltic in 1558, only to have his forces routed by a much smaller Swedish army (1700). There followed a long Swedish campaign of attrition against Augustus of Saxony which ended in 1706 with his deposition from the Polish throne. Meanwhile, the resilient Tsar Peter had revitalised his armed forces. By 1704 Narva was in Russian hands and the foundations of St Petersburg were being constructed at the mouth of the river Neva in the eastern Baltic. In late June 1709 at the Battle of Poltava, a fortress in the Ukraine nearer the Black Sea than the Baltic, the Swedish empire suffered a fatal blow. The Russian victory at Poltava signalled a dramatic shift in the balance of power in the Baltic and eastern Europe. That shift was underlined five years later when Peter's new Baltic fleet defeated the Swedish fleet at the battle of Hangö.

By this time the western powers, particularly the English and the Dutch, were becoming concerned at the changing power structure in the north. In 1702 Peter had attempted to negotiate an alliance with France, assuring Louis XIV that if the French king would help him to secure a Baltic port, the Tsar would build a fleet capable of steering all the Baltic trade towards France. Louis did not respond and in 1706 Peter approached England, this time seeking a favourable response by offering *not* to keep a large fleet on the Baltic. On this occasion too his approaches were ignored. It appears that in the early stages of the War of the Spanish Succession the protagonists all preferred to exclude Muscovy from the European system. By the end of that war, however, the vacuum created by the collapse of the Swedish empire rendered such a policy dangerous. The prized naval stores of the Maritime Powers were once more at risk. In 1716 the British secretary of state for northern affairs complained that naval stores were at such a low level, thanks to 'the knavery of the Muscovites',[3] that there was a danger of the

22

Royal Navy being rendered totally useless in the following year. By then British interest in the Great Northern War had grown even keener, for in 1714 the Elector of Hanover, whose electorate bordered the Swedish possessions of Bremen and Verden, had become King George I of Britain (1714–27).

5

The French succession

The effects of Utrecht

The Peace of Utrecht was chiefly the work of English and French diplomats. The central plank of that settlement was the international recognition and guarantee by the signatories, who included the five great powers of France, the Emperor, Britain, the United Provinces and Spain, of the Protestant succession in Britain and of a French succession which excluded Philip V of Spain. At Queen Anne's death in 1714 the Protestant succession passed to the Elector of Hanover, George I. When Louis XIV died in the following year he was succeeded by his five-year-old great-grandson, Louis XV (1715–74), who was his closest direct descendant in the senior line. A regent was appointed to govern on the young King's behalf, Philip Duke of Orléans. The Utrecht settlement had stipulated that, as the late King's nephew, Orléans should become heir to the throne until Louis XV produced a successor. Philip V, as Louis XIV's second grandson, had been eliminated from the succession by the treaty although according to French fundamental law he should have taken precedence over Orléans. The French succession, therefore, was a crisis waiting to happen, for Philip V did not disguise his intention of claiming the French throne in the event of Louis XV's early death.

Since the two beneficiaries of the Utrecht interpretation of legitimate succession were in power in their respective countries from 1715, the likelihood of some kind of *rapprochement* between the former enemies increased. However, it would be a mistake to assume that Orléans conducted his foreign policy with only his own interests in mind. As regent he was determined to maintain and safeguard the authority of the young king under his charge, Louis XV, and that meant subordinating the interests of his house to those of his sovereign. He took very seriously too the possibility of the restoration of the house of Stuart to the British throne until the disastrous failure of the 1715 rebellion. He also worked hard to avoid a rift with Philip V. Indeed, it was rather Madrid's hostility to the regent than any desire on Orléans's part to protect his own position as heir to the throne that led him in 1717 to sign the Triple Alliance of the Hague with the two Maritime Powers.

We can interpret this treaty as one element in an elaborate framework designed by post-Utrecht diplomats to support the fragile peace. This consisted of a series of mutual guarantees which together offered a form of collective security. The process may be seen as going further than the limited succession guarantees of Utrecht; alternatively, it can be viewed as a reversion to the idea of mutual guarantees formulated in the two partition treaties of 1698 and 1700. Before the signing of the Triple Alliance, the Treaty of Westminster (1716) had been negotiated between Britain and the Emperor. By its terms Britain guaranteed the Emperor's territorial possessions as agreed at Utrecht and promised the aid of a British fleet to resist Spanish attacks upon the emperor's Italian possessions. In return, Leopold reiterated his guarantee of the Hanovarian succession and promised his support for King George's electoral interests in the Baltic.

The Triple Alliance provided for the expulsion of the Old Pretender from France and the destruction of the fortifications at Dunkirk and the neighbouring harbour of Mardyk, havens for French privateers. It also confirmed the signatories' support for the articles in the Treaty of Utrecht relating to the British and French successions and guaranteed reciprocal support, military, naval or financial, should those articles be challenged.

Both the Treaty of Westminster and the Triple Alliance of the Hague underline the existence of a new and significant fact in international relations at this time, namely that the Elector of

Hanover was also King of Great Britain and Ireland. Although the two roles were separate the British government would find it impossible henceforth to ignore the King's Hanoverian interests. Consequently British foreign policy became more responsive to pressures in northern and eastern Europe. The final success of the Anglo-French negotiations leading to the Triple Alliance owed something to George I's belief that France, a traditional ally of Sweden and also on good terms with Muscovy, would be a useful ally in protecting Hanover against the unpredictable Tsar Peter's armies, currently wintering in neighbouring Mecklenburg.

In fact, Tsar Peter was about to visit France, a journey he had sought in vain to make while Louis XIV was king. His aim was to persuade the regent that the French subsidies directed towards Stockholm would be better employed in St Petersburg. Orléans was unwilling to take such a firm position at a time of great uncertainty in the Baltic world. However, the Treaty of Amsterdam (1717), signed between France, Russia and Prussia, contained additional guarantees of the Utrecht settlement by the two northern powers and the promise of French mediation to end the Great Northern War. Though of relatively minor significance, it did contribute to the further stabilisation of European relations. During the remaining years of the war French diplomacy played an important role in the courts of northern Europe, though always in collaboration with Britain. That *entente* was also central to developments in southern Europe and led to the next major international commitment to the principle of collective security.

So long as the Emperor, Charles VI, continued to deny Philip V's right to the Spanish crown and Philip persisted in his plans to regain lost Italian possessions, the danger of a renewal of widespread European conflict remained. Matters came to a head in mid-1717 when a Spanish force invaded Sardinia. English and French diplomats, headed by the two old adversaries Earl Stanhope and the Abbé Dubois, met in London to seek a comprehensive settlement. By June 1718 the two governments were ready to sign a draft convention which stipulated the following: the Emperor was formally to renounce his claim to the Spanish throne and to add his guarantee of the lines of succession in Britain and France established at Utrecht; Philip V was to return Sardinia to the Emperor, who would in turn relinquish it to the Duke of Savoy, Victor Amadeus, in exchange for Sicily; the children of Philip V and his second wife, Elizabeth Farnese, were to become heirs to Parma and Tuscany, where the Farnese family had dynastic claims. Both the Emperor and the King of Spain were to have three months in which to sign the convention. In the event of one or both of them failing to sign, Britain and France undertook to implement these propositions by force. The Emperor accepted the terms and the Treaty of London, the Quadruple Alliance, was signed on 2 August 1718. In fact, at the last moment the Dutch decided not to join Great Britain, France and the Emperor, but the title Quadruple Alliance was justified by the adherence of Savoy to the treaty.

This treaty and its aftermath marked a further advance in the principle that the establishment of international stability justified the setting aside – by force if necessary – of the preferences of small states and their rulers. Thus Victor Amadeus of Savoy had no alternative but to exchange Sicily for Sardinia, and the Grand Duke of Tuscany no voice in the succession to his inheritance. Philip V of Spain was faced with a particularly painful dilemma: whether to accept the terms dictated to him by his rival for the French throne or to take up arms against his own Bourbon relatives. He chose the latter. The subsequent brief war was disastrous for Spain. The Spanish fleet was destroyed by the British navy off Cape Passaro in the western Mediterranean (1718) and in the following year the Spanish army suffered a series of setbacks against French troops in north-west Spain. In February 1720 Spain was forced to accede to the Quadruple Alliance.

By then the strong Franco-British axis, which at this time was the key factor in international relations, had come close to ending the Great Northern War. Not that Britain and France saw eye to eye on all Baltic matters. The complication of the addition of Hanover to Britain's responsibilities caused friction between the two great powers. George I was suspicious of French links with both Sweden and Russia. Early in 1719 Hanover, the Emperor and Augustus II of Saxony/Poland signed a treaty in Vienna aimed against Tsar Peter I which was kept secret from France, an agreement which came close to destroying the Franco-British *entente*. However, later in the same year the French used their good offices to persuade Sweden to relinquish Bremen and Verden to Hanover. At the same time they provided subsidies to enable Sweden's Baltic fleet to challenge Russia's. This was in response to pressure from their British allies, whose naval and commercial interests in the region were threatened by Peter's growing naval power. Eventually French diplomatic mediation led to the Treaty of Nystad (1721), which finally brought the Great Northern War to an end. By the terms of this treaty between Sweden and Russia Peter acquired Livonia, Estonia, Ingria and parts of Karelia, and thereby the eastern and south-eastern Baltic seaboard from Viborg in the Gulf of Finland to Riga on the river Dvina. Sweden had already made peace, in 1719 and 1720, with Hanover, Prussia and Denmark. By successive treaties of Stockholm Hanover obtained Bremen and Verden in northern Germany (1719); and in February 1720 Prussia received most of western Pomerania, having already acquired the eastern part of Pomerania at Westphalia in 1648. At the Treaty of Fredericksburg (June 1720) Sweden relinquished to Denmark her possessions in Schleswig. Thus most of Sweden's Baltic empire had been lost and with it her significance in international relations. Henceforth the Baltic region was increasingly to be dominated by Russia. Following Nystad a grateful senate bestowed upon the Tsar the title of Peter the Great. That remarkable man had transformed the state of Muscovy, which had previously played virtually no role in European diplomacy, into the Russian empire, a state able to command the attention of all the great powers.

Indeed, after the signing of the Treaty of Nystad France wasted no time in exploring the possibility of embracing Russia as its new ally in the north in place of the declining power of Sweden. Sensitive to Hanoverian interests, however, and to the need to keep in place the Anglo-French *entente*, the regent's representative, now Cardinal Dubois, suggested a triple alliance, to include a marriage agreement between the regent's son and the Tsar's daughter, the future Tsarina Elizabeth, with the former becoming heir to the Polish throne. The Polish succession, disputed between the Swedish nominee, Stanislas Lesczynski, and Augustus II of Saxony, remained unresolved, although at the treaty of Fredericksburg Sweden had been forced to recognise the claims of Augustus. The regent's hopes that Russia, Great Britain and France might sign a treaty of mutual defence and guarantee, based upon the treaties of Utrecht, the Triple Alliance of the Hague, the Quadruple Alliance of London, and Nystad (thereby

28

stabilising the status quo in northern and southern Europe), ended with his death in 1723.

By then, however, Orléans had effected another *rapprochement* which was also calculated to lower the international temperature. In 1721 France and Spain signed a defensive alliance of mutual guarantee, once more reiterating the agreements made at Utrecht and London. This convention became the Triple Alliance of Madrid when Britain joined later in the same year. Its effect was to buttress the structure of mutual guarantees established in Europe since Utrecht by reducing the tension between the two Bourbon states. That uneasy relationship had itself provided the main stimulus for the development of a collective security system. It was the intention of the Bourbon signatories to crown the treaty with a double marriage alliance, the betrothal of Philip V's daughter to Louis XV and of the regent's daughter to the heir to the throne of Spain. The latter wedding duly took place but the three year-old infanta, Maria Anna, returned from Paris unmarried in 1725. This episode once more underlines a paradox of the age. The dynastic principle was still such an important element in international relations that it was threatening its own eclipse. For no schemes of collective security, no efforts to establish a balance of power, could co-exist with rampant dynasticism.

The close relationship between Britain and France after Utrecht prevented a number of potential conflicts from escalating into full-scale war. Both countries needed peace to repair the commercial, financial and psychological damage inflicted by a prolonged period of conflict. Both the King of Great Britain and the French regent were beneficiaries of the settlement at Utrecht and naturally inclined therefore to support it. Although Orléans's foreign policy was not primarily aimed at furthering his own interests, one aspect might legitimately attract criticism. He was inclined to sacrifice French commercial and colonial interests in order to secure his objectives. The Triple Alliance of Madrid restored to British traders a number of commercial advantages over the French in the Spanish empire. France also returned to Spain the important port of Pensacola in Florida, acquired during the brief war of 1719. Orléans and his chief foreign policy adviser, Dubois, were aware that they were sacrificing French interests to those of the English in particular. They remained insensitive to the growing importance of colonies and overseas trade as an arm of national security. In this regard, however, they largely shared the attitude of their predecessors who also concentrated their attention on continental, military matters. Louis XIV's most abiding achievement was to leave France with secure defensible frontiers. From the French perspective, the acquisition of key citadels like Dunkirk and Strasbourg mattered far more than the expansion of territories overseas.

The balance of power in Europe in 1723

Indeed, it is important at this point to draw attention to the significance of geo-political considerations in international relations. The island kingdom of Great Britain, defended by a powerful navy, was relatively secure. When European rivalries came to be fought out overseas Britain's naval supremacy, though increasingly challenged by Spain and France, enabled her to maintain more effective links with the colonies than her rivals could, though the Hanoverian connection continued to render her vulnerable in Europe. France, conversely, remained the most formidable military power on the continent with secure frontiers and a cohesive land mass far easier to defend than a state composed of separate territorial possessions. In addition, her history and cultural tradition emphasised military virtues, reducing the likelihood of any priority being given to an extra-European role.

The Austrian Habsburg empire provided the pre-eminent example of a state whose far-flung territories, bestowing strength in human and material resources, added nevertheless to its vulnerability against enemies able to threaten one area or another of this great *imperium*. Though it is true that Leopold I built up a formidable Danubian base at the expense of the defeated Turks, the acquisition by his son, Charles VI, of the former Spanish Netherlands and of Milan, Naples and Sicily prevented the Habsburgs from concentrating their power. Only the Habsburg family itself gave a degree of unity to these disparate territories. In an age when the significance of dynasticism in international relations was in decline, the undoubted great power status of the Habsburg empire seemed insecurely based, a perception soon to be reinforced by the question of the Pragmatic Sanction. On the other hand, the Bourbon rulers of

Spain were able to rebuild their inheritance free of the dangerous distractions previously caused by the possession of the Spanish Netherlands and the Italian lands.

In northern Europe, where the collapse of the Swedish empire had dramatically demonstrated the difficulty of protecting over-extended lines of communication, a new force was about to emerge upon the international scene. The Hohenzollern electors of Brandenburg–Prussia had been attempting to unite and unify their lands, scattered across northern and eastern Europe, since the Great Elector's acquisition of eastern Pomerania on the south Baltic shore in 1648. In 1720 King Frederick William I (1713–40) gained western Pomerania. Consequently, only the Polish region of West Prussia, with its important port of Danzig, now separated the consolidated electorate of Brandenburg and its capital city of Berlin from East Prussia, the duchy inherited by the Hohenzollern house in 1525. Further east lay the bulk of Poland, a state rendered powerless by its system of elective monarchy in league with an antiquated social structure. Beyond Poland lay Russia, her vital north-west sea frontier finally secured by Peter the Great's success at Nystad. Henceforth she would be too powerful to ignore, not only in Warsaw and Stockholm, but also in the capitals of western Europe.

Despite these shifts, real and potential, in the international balance of power political crises continued to be expressed in the traditional language of dynasticism. The problem of the Polish succession remained unresolved, and lurking beyond that was the even more serious matter of the Austrian succession.

6

The Austrian succession

Emperor Charles VI had signed the Quadruple Alliance of 1718, which reiterated the order of succession in France and Britain as established at Utrecht, without raising the increasingly urgent issue of who was to succeed him. For Charles, who had no son, was anxious that his eldest daughter, Maria Theresa, should inherit all the Habsburg lands. To this effect he published in 1720 the Pragmatic Sanction, a document of Habsburg private family law ordering the succession in Maria Theresa's favour. Charles then began the task of persuading all the estates in the lands governed by the house of Austria to accept the new law. He was not willing to risk antagonising powerful elements within his own dominions – notably the independently minded Hungarian diet – by making the Austrian succession a matter of international concern before reaching agreement at home. However, during the 1720s this latest succession problem did begin to influence the policies of the international community.

Charles VI has been much criticised by historians for his preoccupation with his family succession and for his willingness to concede real advantages to his rivals in return for their paper guarantees of support for Maria Theresa's claims. However, it has to be borne in mind that the Emperor had been a signatory to several international agreements which had at their heart paper guarantees, whether of the French, British or Spanish succession. He was not, in other words, out of step with his contemporaries in seeking to protect the interests of his house by means of international guarantees. What made Charles's position increasingly vulnerable was the nature of the Habsburg inheritance. It possessed no common ethnic, linguistic or geographical unity. Its subjects, Czechs, Slovaks, Austrians, Germans, Hungarians, Italians and Netherlanders, shared no common socio-economic structure. There was no unified nobility of the sort emerging in Russia and Prussia, committed to the dynasty's service. The Habsburgs' subjects were foreigners to each other and most of them to their sovereign. That fact would have mattered less a century earlier. But by the eighteenth century, despite the rhetoric to the contrary, dynastic policies were ceasing to command the field. This was partly because the increasing size and expense of armies and navies were beginning to make national security the paramount issue. That fact itself was bound to diminish the significance of dynastic politics. In addition, most of the important states in early eighteenth-century Europe had the geo-political capacity to seek and secure frontiers and then to defend them. The great exception was the house of Habsburg. For the very fact that its scattered lands were united only by its common sovereign meant that in Vienna dynastic policies had to remain paramount. That was the crucial difference of perception between Charles VI and his fellow monarchs as the problem of the Austrian succession loomed.

Spain was the first of the powers to guarantee the Pragmatic Sanction. After the death of the Duke of Orléans France's new chief minister, the Duke of Bourbon, reneged upon the earlier marriage treaty which would have led to the marriage of Louis XV to the King of Spain's daughter, Maria Anna. Instead he arranged for Louis to marry Maria Leszcynska, the daughter of Stanislas Leszcynski, one of the claimants to the Polish throne. This decision led to the breaking off of diplomatic relations between France and Spain. It also encouraged Philip V to seek an agreement with the Emperor. The result was the first Treaty of Vienna (1725). The terms of this treaty were less significant than the reaction in western capitals to the news of its signing. The Emperor conceded nothing beyond reiterating his agreement, already incorporated in the Quadruple Alliance, that Philip's two sons by his marriage to Elizabeth Farnese should in due course succeed in Parma and Tuscany. However, he refused to allow Spanish garrisons to be established there as Philip had

33

demanded. In return Spain guaranteed the Pragmatic Sanction and promised that the Emperor's Ostend Company would be allowed to trade on the same conditions as those enjoyed by the two Maritime Powers in every part of the Spanish empire except the Americas. The Ostend Company, set up in 1722 to trade between the Austrian Netherlands and the Far East, enjoyed an immediate success and attracted the enmity of the Dutch and the British, whose East India companies had long monopolised that trade. Finally, the two signatories to the first Treaty of Vienna promised mutual assistance in the event of attack.

Although the agreement reached at Vienna was unremarkable, it seemed to French and British ministers to represent an important new departure. For in place of the community of interest fashioned by the Franco-British *entente* and held together in an admittedly fragile way by a network of mutual guarantees, a situation of mutual hostility between two armed camps seemed to be emerging. For the Emperor and the King of Spain had been adversaries since their rival candidature for the Spanish succession. Merely by signing a separate treaty they were threatening the carefully constructed stability of Europe. The British and French responded later in the same year with the alliance of Hanover, to which Prussia was a signatory, an indication both of the vulnerability of Hanover and of the fear in the west of further Russian expansion following Peter the Great's success at Nystad.

In the following year (1726) Russia joined the first Treaty of Vienna. Following Peter the Great's death (1725) the Russian Empire had entered a period of domestic instability, but the size of her army, well in excess of 200,000 men, made her a significant military power and a valuable ally. This alliance admitted Russia to the higher ranks of the European diplomatic system, thereby bestowing upon her a status which had been denied to Peter the Great. The Austro-Russian link in particular was to prove surprisingly durable, becoming a stable element in international relations for much of the remainder of this period. As a *quid pro quo* for her admission to the top diplomatic table Russia recognised the Pragmatic Sanction. One of the first results of the Austro-Russian alliance was to persuade King Frederick William I of Prussia to leave the alliance of Hanover, keenly conscious as he was of the vulnerability of East Prussia

34

to a hostile Russia. In 1726 he too guaranteed the Pragmatic Sanction and moved in the direction of the Austro-Russian bloc.

Thus far the Emperor had succeeded adroitly in extracting support for the succession of his daughter, Maria Theresa, from Spain, Russia and Prussia at no cost to his own interests. The risk he had taken was of dividing Europe into two mutually hostile groupings, and thereby significantly increasing the danger of renewed and widespread European conflict.

The coming together in one camp of Austria, Russia and Prussia provides the first clear indication of a shift in Europe's centre of gravity from the west to the east–centre, where the military might of these three powers was concentrated. This was to become a factor of increasing significance as the century progressed.

In the short term, however, there was little appetite for war in Europe. In France the inept Duke of Bourbon was replaced in 1726 by the young King's former tutor, the remarkable Cardinal Fleury, who took up the reins of foreign policy at the age of seventy-three and only relinquished them shortly before his ninetieth year. Fleury favoured a pacific policy, though never at the expense of French interests. Britain took a rather more aggressive line towards Charles VI, particularly over the Ostend Company, whose shipping the Maritime Powers began to seize in 1727. Even more bellicose was the maverick Philip V of Spain, who in the same year laid siege to the island of Gibraltar, lost to Britain at the Utrecht settlement of 1713–14. That these actions did not lead to full-scale war owed much to the subtle diplomacy of Cardinal Fleury as well as to the fact that the Emperor also favoured peace. Charles viewed his links with Madrid with increasing disfavour and was prepared to acquiesce in Fleury's plan to pacify Europe along lines established earlier in the Quadruple Alliance of 1718. The Preliminaries of Paris (1727), reaffirming the terms of the Quadruple Alliance and suspending the Ostend Company's trading, were signed by Britain, the United Provinces, France and Austria. As in 1718, Spain at first refused to join this powerful coalition, only to be forced to adhere by the Convention of the Pardo (1728).

For the moment, therefore, the interests of the great powers remained sufficiently in tune to enable them to reassert the concert of Europe. But for how long could it survive when its fragility had been so recently demonstrated? Two questions in

35

particular have to be examined. How secure was the Anglo-French alliance which for so long had been the key element in stabilising the international situation? And what would be the repercussions of the Emperor's determination to ensure his eldest daughter's succession in all his dominions? Neither Britain nor France had yet guaranteed the Pragmatic Sanction.

In fact, the pressures which had originally persuaded the French and British governments of the need for close co-operation no longer existed. King Louis XV now had an heir, a son born in 1729, so that the French succession was less likely to depend upon the guarantee of the Utrecht settlement. Similarly, in Britain the threat of a Jacobite restoration which would overturn the Hanoverian line seemed increasingly remote. France, her economy and morale restored by over a decade of peace, had less need of the alliance which Britain for its part regarded as a convenient, temporary policy which would in changing circumstances lose its appeal. Indeed, there were many in Britain who continued to view the French as the real enemy, 'political, maritime, colonial and commercial competitors'.[4] What most concerned British ministers, however, headed by Sir Robert Walpole, was the continued security of Hanover. There is no reason to suggest that when Walpole decided to open discussions with Vienna without informing Cardinal Fleury he intended to bring Franco-British collaboration to an end. On the contrary, it was because he did not doubt French willingness to continue to play a part in the defence of Hanover that he sought similar assurances from Austria which, along with her allies, Russia and Prussia, had threatened Hanoverian security on a number of occasions during the 1720s.

The second Treaty of Vienna was signed in 1731 between the Emperor and George II, the latter as King of Great Britain (1727–60) and Elector of Hanover. Each guaranteed the possessions of the other. The Emperor also agreed to suppress the Ostend Company and to allow Don Carlos, Philip V's son, to enter Italy as Duke of Parma. This latter clause enabled Spain to accede to the treaty, which the Dutch also joined in the following year. Both these powers, and Britain, duly guaranteed the Pragmatic Sanction.

The second Treaty of Vienna marked the end of the Anglo-French *entente*. Fleury was greatly irritated by the clandestine fashion in which Walpole had negotiated with Vienna. Neither was he willing to accede to a treaty which would have required French recognition of the Pragmatic Sanction without the possibility of any *quid pro quo* to take account of France's own interests. This was a particularly sensitive matter in Versailles, where it was common knowledge that the Archduchess Maria Theresa was to marry the Duke of Lorraine. The incorporation of Lorraine into the hereditary Habsburg lands would have driven a wedge deep into France's most vulnerable eastern frontier. Walpole's desire to protect his sovereign's electorate brought to an end a period of relative tranquillity in European international relations.

After 1731 Europe became a more dangerous place. Following the Peace of Utrecht the former warring states had come together out of a shared sense of weakness. That phase had now passed, and with the dissolution of the Franco-British alliance the way was open for strong powers to pursue their own interests with unpredictable results. Just as a generation earlier Europe had contemplated the partition of the Spanish Habsburgs' empire, so in the 1730s speculation grew that a similar fate might await their Austrian cousins. Within the Holy Roman Empire the Elector of Bavaria opposed the Pragmatic Sanction. He was married to a daughter of the Emperor Joseph I, the elder brother of Charles VI, and through his wife had territorial ambitions in Austria. The most powerful continental state, France, still refused to guarantee the Pragmatic Sanction, and amongst those who had done so it was impossible to anticipate how their situation might force them to act when Charles VI eventually died. His allies included Russia and Prussia, both states capable of making a significant military impact. Indeed, their growing importance on the geo-political map of Europe was shortly to be demonstrated by the corresponding weakness of their common neighbour Poland. Before the final drama of the Austrian succession was played out from 1740, the prologue was announced in 1733 with the death of Augustus II, Elector of Saxony and King of Poland.

7

The Polish succession

International implications

The vast commonwealth of Poland–Lithuania which stretched from the Baltic almost to the Black Sea had been in decline for nearly two centuries. In 1572 the principle of elective monarchy had been introduced into Poland. The effect was to make the Polish nobility virtually independent of the crown. As election followed election, the rights of the monarchy were increasingly dismantled and the nobility acquired the power to veto any reform, however necessary in the national interest, which it could be argued threatened its liberties. By the eighteenth century this once great east European state had lost the capacity to take independent or coherent action. It was incapable of raising a large army or even of employing a diplomatic corps to monitor the international scene. Poland's vulnerability both fascinated and concerned its neighbours. For the security of Russia, Prussia and Austria was bound up with the insecurity of the Polish commonwealth.

After the victory of Poltava over the Swedes (1709) Peter I restored Augustus II of Saxony to the Polish throne and effectively turned Poland into a client state. That situation was maintained by means of the Russian army and by the introduction in 1716 of a Russian guarantee of the Polish constitution, a device which permitted Russian intervention at any time in order to maintain the enfeebled political status quo.

In 1733 Augustus II died and a new election had to take place. There were two candidates. The first was Stanislas Lesczynski, the Polish nobleman who had been elected earlier in 1704 with the support of Charles XII of Sweden before being replaced by Augustus II. His situation had changed substantially by 1733 for he had become the father-in-law of Louis XV of France, his daughter Maria having married the King in 1725. There was an obligation, therefore, upon the French government on dynastic grounds alone to support Stanislas's candidature. However, a broader security preoccupation also influenced French policy. The concentration of an allied military bloc in east–central Europe concerned the policy-makers at Versailles, as did the threat nearer home of the possible absorption of Lorraine into the Habsburg Empire. There was a strand in French foreign policy at this time favourable to the partition of the Habsburg empire if the opportunity presented itself. Just such an opportunity might have been one result of a disputed Polish succession.

The second candidate was the late King's son, also Frederick Augustus, the new elector of Saxony. His candidature was supported by the Emperor and Russia. In September 1733, the Polish diet elected Stanislas as king for the second time. The opposition's immediate response was an invasion by the Russian army which forced Lesczynski to flee his new capital. On 5 October a new diet, heavily influenced by the presence of Russian troops, elected the Elector of Saxony as Augustus III, King of Poland (1733–63). Five days later France declared war on Austria.

France had not been idle during the preceding months of 1733. She first turned her attention to northern Italy and by the Treaty of Turin (September 1733) promised to assist Charles Emmanuel, King of Sardinia and Duke of Savoy, in wresting the Milanese from the Emperor's grasp. Her diplomatic negotiations with Spain then resulted in the signing of the Treaty of the Escorial (November 1733), usually known as the first Family Compact. By its terms France guaranteed to Don Carlos possession of Parma and Tuscany and promised to assist his younger brother Don Philip to acquire from the Emperor Naples and Sicily. Austrian power in Italy was to be destroyed. The two countries also guaranteed each other's territories in Europe and overseas. The perceived threat of British expansion against the colonial empires of both countries had persuaded them of the need to co-operate in that theatre. Finally, France's preferred German ally, Charles Albert, Elector of Bavaria, was paid a subsidy to ensure his neutrality.

It is important not to be misled by the rhetoric surrounding these events. The dynastic overtones of the 'Polish succession', and particularly of the Treaty of the Escorial, which proclaimed 'a perpetual and irrevocable Family Compact',[5] disguise a French preoccupation with security in a changing world. That concern was focused both narrowly, upon the duchy of Lorraine, and more strategically, upon the threat posed by her old Habsburg antagonist and by British imperial power. In the light of the logistical problems involved there was no possibility of Stanislas Lesczynski being supported on the Polish throne by the power of French arms. France's interests were much closer to home, in Italy and on her eastern frontier. It is significant that although the aggressor in Poland was Russia it was against the Emperor that France declared war.

The War of the Polish Succession

The Russian troops had little difficulty in overrunning Poland. Stanislas fled to the port of Danzig, where he was joined by a token French expeditionary force which was easily defeated. From that moment Augustus III's succession to the Polish throne was secure. Further west, French troops crossed the Rhine and also moved into northern Italy. In 1733 the key province of Lorraine was seized and a Franco-Savoyard army took Milan. In the following years Spanish forces took Naples and Sicily. That was the end of serious conflict although peace was not finally signed for a further four years. The terms of the third Treaty of Vienna (1738) were a triumph for France and for Fleury's low-key but highly effective approach. The Cardinal had succeeded in keeping Britain out of the war partly because of his studied moderation. He did not, for example, threaten the Austrian Netherlands or Hanover, aware of the fact that a move against either state would have forced the Maritime Powers to intervene. He was therefore able to fashion a settlement that not only restored French hegemony in western Europe but also began the process of partitioning the Habsburg empire and marginalising Britain's European role. For, despite the guarantee of the Pragmatic Sanction given in the second Treaty of Vienna (1731), Britain failed to support Charles VI during the war, thus enabling Fleury adroitly to mend his fences with the Emperor as soon as hostilities ceased. An Austro-French agreement was signed in October 1735.

The terms of the third Treaty of Vienna, essentially dictated by France, were as follows: Lorraine was to be handed over to the unsuccessful candidate for the Polish succession, Stanislas Lesczynski, who would rule there during his lifetime. After his death the duchy would be incorporated through transmission to his daughter, Maria, Louis XV's queen, into the French state. This familiar dynastic mechanism masked French determination to secure the eastern frontier, an ambition which even the great Louis XIV had failed to achieve but which was finally realised upon Stanislas's death in 1766. The powerlessness of dynasticism in the face of realpolitik was becoming ever more apparent. Francis, Duke of Lorraine, had married Maria Theresa the future Empress, in 1736. To compensate for the loss of the duchy over which his family had ruled for many generations he was transferred to the former Medici fief of Tuscany. That was despite the provision in the recently signed Family Compact that Tuscany should be inherited by the son of Elizabeth Farnese, Don Carlos. The latter's reward for Spanish support during the War of the Polish Succession was the kingship of the Two Sicilies (Naples and Sicily), provided that this Italian kingdom should never be united to Spain. In the north of Italy Charles Emmanuel of Savoy/Sardinia acquired part of the Milanese in return for his military support, and Parma and Piacenza (the other territories claimed by the Farnese as a family inheritance) went to Austria. In Poland Augustus III's kingship was confirmed.

To seal this agreement France finally added her guarantee of the Pragmatic Sanction. However, it was not the Sanction guaranteed earlier by the other great powers. Though still well established in northern Italy the Emperor had lost his domination of the peninsula, with the Spanish Bourbons now strongly entrenched in the south and Savoy in the north. The states of Italy had been reallocated, as Louis XIV had sought to reallocate them in the two partition treaties of 1698 and 1700, in order to safeguard France's security. For the same reason Louis XIV had also intended in the second of those treaties to acquire Lorraine in exchange for Milan. In 1738 Fleury finally achieved an even more advantageous exchange, Lorraine in return for French recognition of Augustus III's kingship of Poland (the latter an acquisition about which France could in any case have done very little). The new arrangements were duly recognised by Great Britain, the Dutch Republic, Spain and Don Carlos, the new King of the Two Sicilies.

The subtle Cardinal Fleury had achieved a remarkable success in restoring France's position as the leading power in Europe at so little cost. Shortly after the Vienna treaty he enjoyed his final triumph as mediator of the peace signed at Belgrade in 1739 between Russia and Austria on the one hand and the Ottoman Turks on the other. In this war, which had been fully engaged in 1737, the allies had fared unequally, Russia enjoying success in Moldavia and the Crimea, Austria being defeated and Belgrade besieged. By 1739 all sides were ready to make peace and to accept French mediation. The Treaty of Belgrade restored Turkish security around the Black Sea and held back the advance of Russia and Austria in the region. Having lost her influence in Poland, it was important for France to regain her previously strong diplomatic position in Constantinople in order to offset the power of the Austro-Russian bloc. At Belgrade she succeeded in this objective, to the benefit of her trading links with the eastern Mediterranean.

These gains were at Britain's expense. Under Walpole Britain had chosen to pursue a policy of neutrality during most of the 1730s precisely in order to concentrate on international trade and commerce. The loosening of her links with continental Europe reflected the fact that the need for collective security which had characterised the period immediately after Utrecht was no longer strongly felt. That essentially defensive idea remained effective only while all the major participants felt the need to avoid conflict. By the 1730s there was no such binding necessity. Britain therefore reverted to a policy of neutrality. Ultimately, her security and prosperity depended upon the power of her navy so there was much to be said for allowing her rivals to exhaust themselves in military adventures. By the end of the decade, however, this strategy appeared to have failed, for her arch-rival France was again threatening to upset the military balance of power in Europe and the Bourbon family alliance was casting a shadow over Britain's commercial and colonial ambitions. In Britain criticism of the peace policy amongst opposition politicians and the press was focused increasingly upon Spain's vigorous efforts in the West Indies to exclude British merchants from her South American trade. The Spaniards proved intransigent and eventually, in October 1739, Britain declared war against Spain. This War of Jenkins's Ear (named after a British sea captain allegedly mistreated by Spanish coastguards) was an attempt to break Spain's trading monopoly with her South American colonies and to dominate Caribbean trade. It seemed poised to escalate into a full-scale colonial and trade war between Britain and the two Bourbon powers. However, it was quickly overtaken by events on the European mainland which were to plunge the great powers into several decades of war.

The War of the Austrian Succession

In May 1740 King Frederick William I of Prussia died and was succeeded by his son, Frederick II (1740–86). In October of the same year the deaths occurred of both the Holy Roman Emperor and head of the house of Habsburg, Charles VI, and shortly afterwards of Anna, who had been Tsarina of Russia since 1730. The only connection between these three events was their timing, yet that was sufficient to provoke a profound shift in the European balance of power and to initiate a further stage in the evolution of modern statecraft. The juxtaposition of these three deaths provides a salutary reminder of the fact that forecasting the future can be no part of the historian's brief.

Though he inherited his father's pledge, Frederick II had not guaranteed the Pragmatic Sanction. He had, however, also inherited a well-trained and equipped army of 80,000 men and a belief, founded upon the neostoical traditions embraced by his predecessors, that any opportunity to strengthen and secure the state should be seized. In October 1740 he found himself facing the inexperienced and insecure empress, Maria Theresa, whose inheritance depended upon the willingness of the great powers to honour their guarantees and whose most steadfast ally since 1726, Russia, was about to be plunged into the chaos of a

43

minority government and a disputed succession. In the winter of 1740 Frederick II invaded the Austrian province of Silesia.

The Prussian king could lay some hereditary claim to parts of Silesia but neither Frederick nor his contemporaries had any doubt about his real motive for the invasion. Silesia was a highly populated province, a fertile land rich in mineral resources and strategically placed. Its acquisition would add to Prussia's security in Germany and weaken the power of her chief rival, Austria. That was sufficient justification, outweighing any other consideration. Frederick's willingness to recognise the primacy of realpolitik for what it was became even clearer in the international negotiations which followed the outbreak of the Silesian war. The wider War of the Austrian Succession which was precipitated by, and enveloped, the First Silesian War, brought France once more to centre stage. The aged and pacific Cardinal Fleury no longer dominated French foreign policy. That role was now being played by the more bellicose Marshal Belle-Isle. The Prussian victory over the Austrians at Mollwitz in April 1741 persuaded France that partition of the Austrian empire was indeed possible. A Franco-Prussian treaty, the first Treaty of Breslau, was signed in June 1741, guaranteeing French support for Prussia's acquisition of Silesia. Charles Albert of Bavaria and Augustus III, the Elector of Saxony, joined the alliance. The former was to become Emperor and King of Bohemia, the latter King of Moravia. With the support of French troops Charles Albert was duly crowned king in Prague and early in 1742, at Frankfurt, he was crowned Holy Roman Emperor as Charles VII (1742–5), the first non-Habsburg to hold that title for three hundred years.

Yet even as Frederick continued amicable diplomatic discussions with his new French ally he was secretly negotiating with Maria Theresa the infamous Convention of Kleinschnellendorf (October 1741), which would bring a temporary halt to the Silesian war, leaving his erstwhile allies France and Bavaria to face the Austrian forces without Prussian support. This was not the end of Frederick's diplomatic treachery for by May 1742 he was once more at the head of his troops, defeating the Austrian forces at the Battle of Chotusitz. In the following month, however, he signed the second Treaty of Breslau with Maria Theresa, enabling Prussia to withdraw from the war with sovereignty over Silesia.

The War of the Austrian Succession still had six years to run. Those years were largely characterised by unprofitable restatements of old rivalries, the indecisive results of which merely underlined their essential irrelevance. In Italy, an old Bourbon–Habsburg fighting ground, the offer of British subsidies persuaded the Austrians into alliance with the scavenging Charles Emmanuel, Duke of Savoy and King of Sardinia, against the French and the Spanish Bourbon ruler of Naples and Sicily, Don Carlos. This move led to the signing of the second Family Compact, the Treaty of Fontainebleau, in October 1743, between France and Spain. The Italian campaign was marked by shifts in Savoy's alliances which were comparable with King Frederick of Prussia's more notorious double-dealing. Charles Emmanuel had originally intended to adopt an anti-Austrian stance until the prospect of acquiring Piacenza and more of the Milanese from Austria was dangled before him. In 1745 the Bourbons defeated his forces at Bassignano and for a brief period afterwards he toyed with the French offer to become king of Lombardy and leader of a north Italian federation, before reverting to the Austrian camp. His reward at the Peace of Aix-la-Chapelle (1748) was a further strip of the Milanese. By and large the war in Italy ended without significant change to the status quo, whereby the peninsula remained broadly divided between Spanish Bourbon influence in the south (Naples and Sicily) and continuing Habsburg power in the north (most of Milan and Tuscany). That was despite the fact that Elizabeth Farnese's younger son, Don Philip, acquired the family inheritance of Parma and Piacenza.

The terms revealed at Aix-la-Chapelle were similarly undramatic as they applied to the Rhineland and the Austrian Netherlands, two other traditional theatres of conflict between Bourbon and Habsburg. With Prussia's withdrawal from the war in 1742 British policy was directed towards undermining French power, largely by means of financial subsidy. King George II supported this thrust, though principally in order to secure Hanover. An Anglo-Hanoverian force, the so-called Pragmatic Army, set out for the Austrian Netherlands in the autumn of 1742 and in the following year, under the command of the King/Elector it defeated a French army at Dettingen, east of the Rhine near Frankfurt. However, the French held firm on the Rhine and in 1745 regained the offensive in the Austrian Netherlands, where Marshal Saxe won the Battle of Fontenoy.

In the same year Charles Edward, the Young Pretender, landed in Scotland and proclaimed the restoration of the house of Stuart. Louis XV promptly recognised him as king of Scotland but withheld recognition of him as king of England until it could be demonstrated that that was the English nation's wish. This cautious approach reflected divisions in France over war strategy. Nevertheless, the invasion was beneficial to French interests since in order to defeat the ill-fated '45', troops had to be withdrawn from the Austrian Netherlands, leaving Marshal Saxe free to consolidate his supremacy there. At Aix-la-Chapelle the status quo was restored. France returned the Austrian Netherlands to Maria Theresa and the barrier fortresses to the Dutch. She again guaranteed the Protestant succession established in Britain and promised to dismantle the naval base at Dunkirk.

In one respect, however, the concluding years of the War of the Austrian Succession restated the fundamental shift which had taken place both in the balance of power in Europe and in the conduct of international affairs. In the summer of 1744, alarmed by the prospect of a Habsburg revival, Frederick II of Prussia rejoined the war and renewed his alliance with France. Although Maria Theresa's authority was boosted by the election of her husband, Francis, Duke of Tuscany, as Holy Roman Emperor (1745–65) following the death of Charles VII in January 1745, she could not withstand the Prussian military machine. Defeats at Hohenfriedberg and Soor forced the Empress to confirm Prussian control of Silesia at the Treaty of Dresden which brought the Second Silesian War to an end in December 1745.

The Treaty of Aix-la-Chapelle which finally brought the War of the Austrian Succession to an end in 1748 touched upon one other issue of momentous significance for the future, the colonial and trading rivalry between Britain and France. The war itself had originated in the commercial disputes centring on the Caribbean. Yet few on either side appreciated the significant shift in power that was taking place. Since the Peace of Utrecht France had rebuilt her naval strength; yet during this war she lost half her ships of the line and around one thousand merchant ships. British command of the sea was assured and the French negotiators at Aix-la-Chapelle were aware of the dramatic decline in trade through French ports as the result of a tightening British naval blockade. Britain, however, was also anxious to secure peace in order to lift the financial burden imposed by the cost of maintaining her own forces and of subsidising her allies. Thus the status quo was restored, including, in India, the return of Madras to Britain, and, in Canada, the return of Louisburg to France. One shrewd observer, the future Duke de Choiseul, destined to be Britain's arch-enemy in the colonial struggle of the 1760s, noted that, having signally failed to resolve the dispute over the boundaries between Acadia and Canada in North America, the treaty would only bring a temporary respite in the quickening struggle for global supremacy.

By the middle of the eighteenth century, therefore, international relations in Europe had indeed reached a watershed. The second half of the century would be dominated by the intense rivalry of two sets of foes, Britain and France and Prussia and Austria, with the unpredictable power of Russia capable of tipping the balance one way or the other. The making of alliances would be governed by these key hostilities and the making of policy would finally dispense with the pretended primacy of dynasticism.

PART II

Portents of change

8

The diplomatic revolution

After the Peace of Aix-la-Chapelle, Anglo-French rivalry continued at a level only just below that of formal hostilities. This was especially true in North America. Indeed, a diplomatic feature of the period before the outbreak of the Seven Years War (1756–63) is the preoccupation in London and Versailles with the effects of policies in America on Europe and vice versa. Outside Europe, both sides sought to provide added security for their colonies. On the borders of Acadia, around Cape Breton and Prince Edward Islands, the British were pushing into Canada and threatening French communications between Louisburg on Cape Breton Island and Quebec on the Saint Lawrence river. Further south, British settlers were seeking to push westwards over the Appalachian mountains. Conversely, French colonial strategy was to link the Canadian territories with French possessions in Louisiana. That involved the establishment of a vast chain of communications beginning with the Great Lakes and extending southwards, by means of a series of forts and settlements in the valley of the Ohio river, to the Mississippi. If successful, such a strategy would threaten the encirclement of Britain's east-coast colonies from Nova Scotia to Georgia. Consequently, despite the formal restoration of peace, relations between the two countries continued to deteriorate. The British view was that the resolution of the conflict in North America was crucial to the balance of power

51

in Europe. In the recently concluded war British naval power had counterbalanced French military successes in Europe and guaranteed British successes in America. If the French were to succeed in their American ambitions, British ministers feared that they would be tempted to resume their efforts to dominate Europe.

This was the hypothesis favoured by the Duke of Newcastle, secretary of state for the northern department until 1754 and then George II's first minister. Newcastle hoped to establish a countervailing set of alliances to deter French aggression in Europe, and he was at the same time willing to act unilaterally against France in America in order to limit French ambitions. His European 'system' included strengthening the barrier fortresses in the Austrian Netherlands, retaining the old alliances with Austria and the Dutch Republic, detaching Spain from France and providing subsidies where necessary to buy support. The Treaty of Aranjuez (1752), by which Austria, Spain and Sardinia guaranteed each other's Italian possessions, was the preliminary to an increasingly pro-British stance in Madrid, an apparent success for one strand of Newcastle's foreign policy.

From mid-1753, when French incursions in the Ohio valley became more systematic, Newcastle favoured military action in America. He was confident that this policy would not lead to war in Europe since at Versailles the peace party was in the ascendant and Spain appeared to be firmly in the British camp. However, by the end of 1754, when Britain was on the point of despatching a strong military force to North America, the diplomatic foundations of the old world began to crumble. In particular, the alliance between London and Vienna, upon which the Duke of Newcastle set great store, seemed less secure. The first intimations of an approaching 'diplomatic revolution' were beginning to appear.

Prince von Kaunitz was the Austrian ambassador in Paris from 1750 until 1753, when he became Maria Theresa's chancellor. He had long favoured a diplomatic *rapprochement* with France, similar to that achieved in the Quadruple Alliance of 1718. His aim was to restore to his Habsburg mistress the province of Silesia, which had remained in Prussian hands after the Treaty of Aix-la-Chapelle (1748). That ambition would be greatly assisted if France could be persuaded to exchange her alliance with Berlin for one with Vienna. For her part, France was becoming increasingly alarmed at British preparations for colonial conflict and was attracted by the possibility of securing her position in Europe by an alliance with Britain's chief continental supporter. Finally, the influence of Russia was again beginning to assert itself on the international stage. Peter the Great's daughter, Elizabeth (1741–62), was now firmly in control of the powerful state bequeathed by her father. Russia and Austria had been allies since 1726. This alliance was reaffirmed in 1746 at St Petersburg, a compact usually referred to as the Two Empresses Treaty between Elizabeth and Maria Theresa. This was a close defensive alliance aimed primarily against Prussia. It included a secret agreement to the effect that if Frederick were to invade Russian or Polish territory Russia would guarantee the restoration of Silesia to the Austrian empire. From this date Elizabeth remained determined to destroy the advancing power of Prussia and to confirm the primacy of Russia's influence in Poland. In 1750 Britain acceded to the Two Empresses Treaty in order to acquire from Austria and Russia a limited guarantee of Hanoverian security against a Prussian attack. These conflicting ambitions raised the level of international tension. However, the diplomatic situation remained fluid until 1755, when the signing of the Anglo-Russian subsidy treaty (the Convention of St Petersburg) provided the catalyst for a series of events which led first to what subsequently came to be called the diplomatic revolution, and then indirectly to the Seven Years War.

As an overseas conflict with France came closer, Britain's concern for the security of Hanover increased, her assumption being that France and Prussia would remain allies. In September 1755, therefore, the Convention of St Petersburg was concluded between Britain and Russia whereby a Russian army of 55,000 men would be made ready to intervene on behalf of Britain or her allies if they or Hanover were attacked. In return Britain agreed an annual subsidy for four years of £100,000 in order to defray the costs of this army-in-waiting. This initiative deeply perturbed Frederick. The King of Prussia was well aware of Elizabeth's animosity towards him and of her determination to persuade Maria Theresa to join her in a declaration of war. Kaunitz, preoccupied with negotiations with Versailles, was anxious in the short term to restrain Russian belligerence. Nevertheless, Frederick had no illusions about the longer-term threat from the two empresses, and the British decision to subsidise the feared Russian army added to his sense of insecurity. He reacted by signing the Convention of Westminster with Britain in January 1756.

This treaty was designed to guarantee the neutrality of the German states. In London, that meant a Prussian obligation to defend Hanover if the electorate were attacked by France; in Berlin a British obligation to come to Frederick's aid if he were attacked by Russia. The effect on French diplomacy of this latest example of Frederick's bad faith was to bring the negotiations with Kaunitz speedily to a conclusion. In May 1726 the first Treaty of Versailles was signed between France and Austria. It was a defensive treaty, as the Convention of Westminster had been, whereby France guaranteed not to attack Austrian territory while Austria promised to remain neutral in the Anglo-French struggle that was just turning to formal war. Each country promised troops or subsidies to the other if attacked by a third party (though the Anglo-French conflict was excluded from the agreement).

With the signing of the first Treaty of Versailles European international relations reached a point of unstable equilibrium. Unofficial sea and colonial warfare between Great Britain and France had already broken out in the summer of 1755, a state of affairs formalised by the British declaration of war on 17 May 1756. Both powers hoped to remain free of continental distractions. Although France had just signed an alliance with Austria, she hoped to avoid involvement in a war against Prussia. Russia, on the other hand, was anxious to attack Frederick but was being restrained by Austria in the hope that the Franco-Austrian *rapprochement* would decisively strengthen the anti-Prussian coalition. Meanwhile, the great powers had established a series of defensive alliances. The Two Empresses Treaty had guaranteed the integrity of Austrian and Russian lands against Prussian assault. The Convention of Westminster guaranteed the neutrality of the German states, and the Treaty of Versailles promised mutual assistance if either signatory was attacked by a third party.

With the loss of the French alliance Frederick the Great felt the noose tightening around his embattled kingdom. He believed rightly that the Tsarina Elizabeth and the Empress Maria Theresa would not postpone their joint assault beyond the following year. He decided therefore to make a pre-emptive strike by invading Saxony at the end of August 1756. Strictly speaking, this action did not automatically convert his enemies' defensive treaties into offensive ones since the electorate of Saxony was not part of either the Russian or the Austrian empire. Nevertheless, its ruler, Augustus III, was an ally of Austria and had been placed on the Polish throne by Russian troops. In addition, Louis XV's son, the Dauphin, was married to the Elector's daughter. Therefore, although Frederick's invasion did not bring an offensive alliance into existence against him forthwith, it brought such an alliance closer. In fact, Russia joined the first Treaty of Versailles in December 1756; in the following month she concluded an offensive agreement with Austria against Prussia; and on 1 May 1757, exactly one year after the first treaty, the second Treaty of Versailles was signed, an offensive alliance between Austria and France.

9

The Seven Years War

This major world conflict in fact consisted of two separate struggles which were nevertheless inextricably linked. Overseas, Britain and France fought their colonial war, and in Europe France, Austria and Russia, joined almost immediately by Sweden and a number of German princes, faced Prussia in what appeared to be a most uneven contest. Prussia owed her survival in part to the inspirational leadership of Frederick, whose exploits at the head of his armies marked him out as a military genius. However, he was also saved by the evident lack of cohesion amongst his enemies, whose motives in going to war were very mixed. Sweden was persuaded by her French ally to intervene in the hope of regaining Pomerania. Her subsequent impact upon the war proved to be negligible. Russia's concern was also with the acquisition of Baltic territory, in this case the duchy of Kurland, and with extending further westwards her frontiers with Polish Livonia and White Russia. Austria's preoccupation was with regaining Silesia. France's motives were complex. Not for the first time, Louis XV and his advisers had been infuriated by Frederick's perfidy in signing the Convention of Westminster, and the temptation to punish this upstart was very strong. Besides, France was still the greatest power in Europe and unlikely to risk losing that position by opting out of a major European conflict. She was, for example, deeply suspicious of Russian ambitions in Poland. Finally, there was the issue of Hanover and of whether losses to Britain overseas might be recouped by successful French sorties into the electorate.

Initially, such a strategy appeared to be unnecessary. The French enjoyed considerable early success against Great Britain. Minorca was seized in 1756, and in North America the key French fortress of Louisburg succeeded in holding out against British attack during 1757. In Europe in the same year French forces defeated the Duke of Cumberland's army of Hanoverian and German mercenaries defending Hanover, at the Battle of Hastenbeck. Cumberland was forced to sign the Convention of Kloster-Zeven, leaving Hanover subject to French occupation. However, the balance began to shift under the driving hand of William Pitt the Elder, the future Earl of Chatham. Under his leadership Britain's domination of the sea became the key to victory. The French Mediterranean and Atlantic fleets were blockaded in port and then decisively defeated at sea in 1759 off Lagos in Portugal and Quiberon Bay in Brittany. It thus became impossible for France to supply and reinforce her colonies. The result was a series of spectacular British victories, which included the capture of Canada, the chief West African centres of the French slave trade to the Caribbean, including the island of Goree, and the West Indian islands of Guadeloupe, Martinique, Dominica, St Lucia, St Vincent and Tobago. In addition, Clive's victory at Plassey (1757) over a local Nawabi force led to the capture of Bengal and thereby to the domination of the whole of the Indian sub-continent.

In Europe, too, the resilient Frederick II was proving capable of holding his own against all expectations. In 1757 he defeated a combined French–imperial force at Rossbach and shortly afterwards at Leuthen an Austrian army almost twice the size of Prussia's. Pitt was encouraged to repudiate the Convention of Kloster-Zeven and to take measures to strengthen the Hanoverian army by the appointment of a new commander-in-chief, Prince Ferdinand of Brunswick, and by the introduction of British reinforcements. Britain also agreed to provide large-scale subsidies for Frederick. In 1758 Ferdinand succeeded in removing the French from Hanover, and his army continued to provide a western buffer for the hard-pressed King of Prussia. French plans to regain lost colonial ground by acquiring a bargaining counter in Europe were finally checkmated.

Meanwhile, the spectacular drama of Frederick the Great's military fortunes continued to be played out. He defeated a Russian army at Zorndorf (1758) but was defeated by the Austrians later in the same year at Hochkirch. In 1759 the Russian victory of Kunersdorf threatened total disaster but Frederick rallied his forces once more to gain a victory over the Austrians at Torgau (1760). Nevertheless, Frederick's position appeared near hopeless, particularly since the Tsarina, Elizabeth, unlike her ally Maria Theresa, remained determined to prosecute the war until the Prussian threat had been totally removed. Frederick was saved by Elizabeth's death and her replacement by Tsar Peter III (1762), who had long been a fervent admirer of the Prussian king. The withdrawal of Russia from the war allowed Frederick and Maria Theresa to make peace at Hubertusburg (1763) on the basis of the restored status quo: Prussia retained Silesia.

The later stages of the Anglo-French struggle were complicated by the entry of Spain into the war as France's ally, following the signing of the third Family Compact in 1761. In 1759 Don Carlos, who had become king of Naples and Sicily in 1738, inherited the Spanish crown as King Charles III (1759–88). Britain's colonial successes against France made the new king fearful for the security of the Spanish empire and persuaded him of the need for Bourbon solidarity in order to prevent the establishment of British colonial hegemony. In the event, however, Spain's intervention merely allowed Britain to increase the tally of her New World conquests, this time at Spain's expense. By the autumn of 1762 France and Spain were both ready to make peace with Britain. The treaty bringing the Seven Years War to an end was signed in Paris in February 1763.

10
The Peace of Paris and its consequences

The significance of the Peace of Paris lay in the unequivocal nature of Britain's victory. France ceded the whole of Canada, including Cape Breton Island, retaining only fishing rights off Newfoundland and in the gulf of the St Lawrence river. She also yielded Louisiana to Spain in compensation for the Spanish loss of Florida to Britain. In the West Indies, Britain acquired the islands of Grenada, Tobago, Dominica and St Vincent. In India, despite the return of Pondicherry to France, Britain's control of Bengal and Madras provided her with the springboard from which to dominate the trade of the sub-continent. In West Africa, France ceded part of the coast and river of Senegal to Britain. Finally, in Europe, she returned Minorca to Britain and to King George III, as elector, all the land belonging to the electorate of Hanover.

Yet the peace of Paris was not well received by all British politicians. In the course of negotiations, as well as restoring Pondicherry to France and permitting the French to retain fishing rights off Canada, the British government returned several other prizes acquired during the war. These included Guadeloupe, Martinique and St Lucia in the West Indies, and the islands of Belle-Isle off the coast of Brittany and Goree off the North African coast, the latter the centre for the traffic in slaves to the French West Indies. The Earl of Chatham, in particular, shared with his arch-rival, the Duke de Choiseul, the belief that Britain and France were engaged in a struggle for global commercial hegemony, and he saw no reason to improve the enemy's ability to prosecute that struggle.

In fact, Britain was on the way to achieving a decisive victory in that conflict, though it is easier for historians to reach that conclusion than it was for contemporaries. The ports of France's Atlantic coast, the key to the health of her mercantile economy, went into decline. No less seriously, French state finances went into permanent deficit. In terms of her international reputation France had suffered a humiliating reduction in status. The result was that after 1763 her tentative experiments in economic and financial reform went hand in hand with the determination to regain prestige at Britain's expense. Paradoxically, when the opportunity presented itself in the War of American Independence (1775–83), France's contribution to the British defeat was achieved at the high cost of destroying the state's financial viability and helping to prepare the way for revolution.

In the early stages of the War of American Independence, France and Spain secretly exported money, arms and gunpowder to the colonists before committing themselves openly to the war, in the case of France from the summer of 1778 and in that of Spain from April of the following year. The Treaty of Versailles (1783), which ended the War of American Independence, appeared to offer the Bourbons some revenge for the losses sustained at the Peace of Paris. Britain had to recognise the independence of her thirteen American colonies, to restore Tobago in the West Indies and the Senegal river in West Africa to France, and to hand back Florida and Minorca to Spain. However, this was a pyrrhic victory for the Bourbons. For although France regained some of her lost international reputation the enormous financial burden she had incurred in the process would ultimately prove fatal to the old regime. Besides, the loss of the American colonies had little effect upon Britain's trading relationship with the new republic. Strong social and cultural ties, as well as long-standing commercial ones, made for a rapid restoration of economic links. Indeed, Britain gained from no longer having to bear the costs of maintaining her North American colonies.

By the 1780s the foreign policy of the European states was no longer based on the principles generally recognised a century earlier. Britain, in particular, had played a major part in changing international perceptions. The significance of her role was centred around the abolition in 1688 of divine-right monarchy and the emergence of a new focus for the citizens' loyalty, the impersonal state of Britain, given human form in the representation of Britannia. Consequently, the idea of patriotism as the subjects' ultimate obligation made its halting appearance during the eighteenth century. It reflected the changing political values which followed the shift in power from the Crown to the House of Commons. In due course, as patriotism spread to a variety of other political regimes, the bases of its appeal shifted. In Britain, however, it was woven out of three intertwined strands: liberty, Protestantism and commerce. To the Protestant men of property who dominated the two houses of parliament after the defeat of the Catholic Stuarts, the acquisition of wealth through foreign and domestic trade represented the best means of maintaining political stability and national security. The people's prosperity permitted the establishment of a formidable naval force, which in turn safeguarded both the interests of the nation and the wealth of the subjects. This aggressive commercial policy, designed to secure and hold world markets, represented a far more expensive national commitment than any of the foreign policy initiatives undertaken by the royal house of Stuart. Indeed, in the second half of the eighteenth century the escalating costs of maintaining armies and navies was testimony to the changing nature of international relations across the continent, though the reasons for change were not those found in Britain. In this regard the diplomacy of central and eastern Europe merits particular attention.

11
The changing balance of power

The growth of state power

During and after the Seven Years War the western powers became increasingly preoccupied with global politics, while the traditional causes of diplomatic dispute, the possession of land and the security of frontiers, were located to the east. That dichotomy is reflected in the statistics of the great powers' naval and military strengths. Both Britain's naval personnel and her tonnage doubled between the age of Louis XIV and the Seven Years War. The size of the Bourbon navies was subject to great fluctuation, though by the time of the War of American Independence France had some eighty ships of the line and Spain around sixty (though together they failed to match the British fleet's total of some one hundred and seventy). By the 1780s the Russian fleet, first established by Peter the Great and then allowed to decline after his death, had been re-established with thirty-seven ships of the line on the Baltic and around twenty on the Black Sea.

It is the growth of Russia's military strength, however, like that of the neighbouring powers of Prussia and Austria, which most reveals the shift of the balance of power in Europe. Between the later years of Peter the Great's reign and the last decade of the century the Russian army more than doubled in size, rising from 200,000 to 450,000 men. The Prussian army, with fewer than 80,000 troops in 1723, reached almost 200,000 during the long reign of Frederick the Great. Finally, the Austrian Habsburg forces, already numbering 165,000 in 1716, were over 300,000 by 1783. By comparison the French army, which in 1710 numbered some 280,000 soldiers, had 100,000 fewer by the end of the Seven Years War.

The cost of this significant increase in military and naval expenditure represented a level of national commitment unthinkable in traditional dynastic terms. Spending on the armed forces in Prussia accounted for two thirds of state revenue by the end of Frederick's reign. It reached 90 per cent in Russia under Peter the Great and did not diminish substantially during the rest of the century. In the Austrian Habsburg empire, too, the costs of the army dominated the economy. The question to be addressed, therefore, is: 'How did the rulers of these territories justify demanding that level of support from their subjects?'

The simple answer is that the need for security, as usual, overrode all other considerations. Russia's frontiers to the south and west brought her into contact with former great powers in decline, the Ottoman empire and Poland. These two states also bordered the Habsburg empire. Prussia too shared frontiers with Poland and with Austria, and her seizure of Silesia from the latter had raised the level of mutual suspicion to a high pitch. By this time something of a power vacuum had developed in eastern and south-eastern Europe, and this, in their quest for security, the dominant powers in the region were seeking to fill. They were all well equipped for this role. Prussia had been built by its Hohenzollern rulers into a formidable military state in which the needs of the army and the values of the military overshadowed all other considerations. Russia, first under Peter the Great and later under Catherine II, the Great (1762–96), began to exploit her enormous resources of manpower, aided by an increasing knowledge of western tactics and technology. In Vienna the loss of Silesia jolted the Habsburg rulers, Maria Theresa and her son Joseph II (1765–90), into reforming their old-fashioned inheritance. Reform and expansion of the army was accompanied by the reorganisation of state finances which in turn necessitated profound social, economic and administrative change. By the final third of the eighteenth century, therefore, the relationships between these three formidable powers were potentially explosive.

63

There is a second, more complex, response to the question of how the rulers of these countries justified the demands made by them upon their subjects. This relates to the influence of the Enlightenment. The roots of that wide-ranging set of ideas which flowered in the middle and later decades of the eighteenth century were to be found, in part at least, in the scientific revolution of the previous century. One of the effects of this revolution was to undermine the authority of divine-right kingship by distancing the Divinity from human affairs. It appeared, for example, that the functioning of the vast universe itself required no supernatural explanation but could be accounted for by observation and mathematical laws. If rulers could no longer justify their authority as representing God's close interest in their subjects' welfare, how was that authority to be maintained? Again part of the answer is to be found in the fall-out from the scientific revolution.

For this new mode of rational enquiry, based upon observation and experiment, encouraged the growth of cameralism. The cameralists were teachers of political economy and public administration in German and imperial universities who, by analogy with the scientists' mechanistic approach to understanding the natural world, sought to uncover and apply the rules governing the working of political society. In the words of a leading cameralist, J. H. G. von Justi, who was a professor in Vienna (1750–53), a properly constituted state must be exactly analogous to 'a machine in which all the wheels and gears are precisely adjusted to one another'; and the ruler must be 'the foreman, the mainspring . . . which sets everything in motion'.[6] For the cameralists, therefore, the state was run by committees, bureaux, inspectors, statisticians, agronomists, that is, by people who could give expert advice and draw up projects whereby that advice might be implemented. There began to emerge the idea of the state machine, presided over by a ruler whose power was no longer primarily patrimonial and judicial but executive and managerial. Therefore Frederick the Great chose to describe himself as the first servant of the state, a description which could equally be applied to Joseph II in the Austrian Habsburg empire and to Catherine II in Russia.

Cameralism had two objectives. First, it aimed to increase national wealth by a more rational and efficient organisation of the state's resources, a significant objective for rulers desperate for the revenue required to support the growing costs of their armed forces. Second, it sought to improve the prosperity and happiness of the subjects. Both objectives were embraced by the rulers of Prussia, Russia and Austria, though it was inevitable that practical considerations would limit the extent to which their plans would be implemented. However, their new role as the managing directors of their states allowed them considerable freedom to regulate and control the lives of their subjects. In that way they were adding to the security of the state and the well-being of the subjects. Natural law theories, which were also a theme of the Enlightenment, added weight to this argument by suggesting that subjects could only aspire to human perfectibility as members of a state. The additional authority acquired by these state guardians, the king of Prussia, the tsarina of Russia and the emperor of Austria, was justified not by moral or legal considerations but simply by its effectiveness in safeguarding interests of state. The concept of realpolitik, or reason of state, which had revealed itself periodically in the history of international relations over the previous century was now free to take centre stage as the ultimate determinant of foreign policy.

The Ottoman empire and the partition of Poland

Catherine II replaced her deposed husband Peter III as ruler of Russia in 1762. Shortly afterwards, with the death of King Augustus III of Poland in 1763, she faced a critical decision. Through the puppet Saxon rulers the Russians had established a stranglehold over Polish affairs. Catherine decided to tighten that control by nominating a former lover, the Polish nobleman Stanislas Poniatowski, as the new king (1764–96). Her recent enemy, Frederick II of Prussia, hastened to join Catherine in a defensive alliance (1764) which both strengthened the new tsarina's position and guaranteed Frederick against any Austrian endeavours to regain Silesia.

Poniatowski, however, proved less malleable as king of Poland than his sponsors intended. He introduced a series of reforms which provoked Catherine into armed intervention. The Poles responded by forming the Confederation of Bar and instituting a campaign of guerrilla warfare in the south of the country close

65

to the borders of the Ottoman empire. The threat thereby posed to the Turks' Balkan possessions led them to declare war on Russia in 1768.

What at first appeared a threatening situation for Russia was transformed by a series of military and naval successes into an opportunity for large-scale gains at the Ottomans' expense. Moldavia, Wallachia and the Crimea were all captured by Russian troops, and in a spectacular manoeuvre a Russian naval force sailed from the Baltic through the straits of Gibraltar and defeated the Turkish fleet at the Battle of Chesmé in the eastern Mediterranean. This turn of events troubled both Russia's old ally, Austria, and her new ally, Prussia. The Habsburgs had long considered the Balkans to be within their sphere of influence and Frederick the Great feared any threat to the delicate balance of power established in the region after the Seven Years War. For her part, Catherine II's demands increased with the successes of her armed forces against the Turks. The result was to force a *rapprochement* between bitter enemies, Prussia and Austria, in an attempt to restore the political equilibrium. It was Frederick the Great who suggested a way out of the dilemma with his scheme for a partition of Poland from which all three powers would benefit, though he only acted after Austrian troops had begun to acquire Polish territory. If she accepted this proposition, Russia would lose the indirect but near total control of Polish affairs which she had exercised for much of the eighteenth century, while Austria, still seeking a *quid pro quo* for the loss of Silesia, would acquire no compensating advantage over Prussia in a tripartite partition. Nevertheless, the differing interests of all three states, sharpened by the apparent crumbling of Ottoman power in the south, persuaded them to sign a series of conventions in St Petersburg in 1772. Under direct threat from Catherine's troops, the Polish diet had no option but to ratify them.

By the first partition Poland lost 30 per cent of her territory and 35 per cent of her population. The largest share of land went to Russia in the form of Livonia and White Russia. Austria received Galicia, an area slightly less than that acquired by Russia but containing twice the population. The smallest territorial gain was Prussia's acquisition of Polish Prussia, though this was of the greatest strategic significance since it joined East

Prussia to the bulk of the Prussian kingdom in northern and central Europe.

The partition of Poland lacked even the pretence of legal justification. Poland was an independent country, whose strategic significance and internal weakness conspired to attract the attention of powerful neighbours determined to protect their own interests. The doctrine of collective security, as it was applied in 1772, differed substantially from the prototype version of 1698 and 1700, when Louis XIV and William III had attempted to partition the Spanish Habsburg empire. Then the legal dynastic claims of the candidates had formed the basis of the partition treaties, even though the threat of force loomed behind the Anglo-French initiative. By 1772 the ability to impose a settlement which protected the interests of the signatories was its own justification. The enormity of the implications of this change was to be demonstrated in the second and third partitions, in 1793 and 1795, when Austria, Russia and Prussia succeeded in removing Poland altogether from the map of Europe.

Meanwhile, Catherine II's First Russo-Turkish War was concluded in 1774 with the Treaty of Kuchuk-Kainardji. This treaty marked an important landmark in Russia's relations with the Ottoman empire, and the beginning of what later came to be known as the Eastern Question. Where Peter the Great's policies had failed, Catherine the Great's succeeded. She acquired a firm hold on the north shore of the Black Sea and the right to free navigation. The Crimea ceased to be subject to the Ottoman empire and became an independent state. However, it was thought to be only a matter of time before it was annexed by Russia, an event which duly took place in 1783. Finally, the Turks recognised Russia's right to intercede on behalf of the Orthodox Christian subjects of the Porte, a significant concession which would be regularly exploited by nineteenth-century Russian governments. It seemed in 1774 that the prospects for Russian expansion in the south against a declining Ottoman empire were rosy. Catherine's Second Russo-Turkish War (1787–92) went some way towards confirming that view. However, the Eastern Question would bedevil international relations in the region for more than a century to come.

The War of the Bavarian Succession (1778–79) and the Armed Neutrality (1780)

The three great powers of east–central Europe continued to eye each other with suspicion in the years after Kuchuk-Kainardji. When the Elector of Bavaria died in 1777 without leaving a direct heir, the Emperor Joseph II, who had been co-regent of the Austrian empire with his mother Maria Theresa since 1765, persuaded the nominated successor, the Elector Palatine, to cede most of Lower Bavaria to the Habsburgs. Here was the long-awaited opportunity for the Habsburgs to gain compensation for the loss of Silesia. Joseph's strategy, comparable with Frederick the Great's in his acquisition of Polish Prussia, was to consolidate the Habsburg lands, in this instance by seizing control of the upper Danube. The language of succession harks back to an earlier period of rival dynastic claims, and Joseph did try to capitalise upon his marriage to the late Elector's sister; but essentially this was part of the power politics of the region. The three chief predators were all conscious of the need to seize an opportunity or at the very least to prevent their rivals from doing so. Consequently, Prussia declared war on the Habsburgs. Hostilities amounted to very little before peace was signed at Teschen (1779). Austria gained a small though not insignificant part of Bavaria which contributed to the linking up of the Habsburg lands without, however, seriously upsetting the balance of power. The real victor was Catherine of Russia who, with the French, was responsible for mediating the peace. Russian influence was thereby considerably enhanced, a fact which helped to persuade the tsarina to undertake a further international initiative.

This was the Armed Neutrality, a league of neutral powers headed by Russia which grew out of Catherine's desire to mediate between Britain and the Bourbon powers of France and Spain in the War of American Independence. The Scandinavian powers, the Dutch Republic, Portugal, Austria and Prussia all joined the league which sought to protect the rights of neutral trade at sea. These rights were held to include the free navigation of neutral ships between the ports of belligerents and the freedom from attack of neutral ships carrying commodities belonging to nations at war. Frederick II and Joseph II were persuaded to join, though both resented their inferior relationship with the increasingly dominant Catherine and each took a hostile view of the other's accession to the league.

At the same time that Prussia was joining the Armed Neutrality, Catherine was negotiating a secret agreement with Joseph II. The Russian ruler had decided that she could best profit from the newly perceived weakness of the Ottoman empire by acting in concert with Austria. Agreement was duly reached and when the Second Russo-Turkish War began in 1787 the Austrians fought as allies of Russia. Thus the so-called 'Northern System', inspired by Catherine's chief diplomatic adviser, Count Nikita Panin, which had been the basis of Russian foreign policy since 1764, was finally discarded. It had been built upon a close alliance with Prussia and was essentially defensive and pacific in intent. By 1781, however, an increasingly confident Tsarina was ready to pursue a more aggressive expansionist policy in the south and to acquire a new ally, Joseph, for the purpose.

Since the French and, to a lesser extent, the Spaniards had expressed their support for the neutrals' principles, the Armed Neutrality acquired an anti-British thrust, though it had little practical effect upon British policy. The league did have the effect, however, of bringing the foreign policy relationships of the whole of Europe, north, south, east and west, back into a single configuration. Since 1763 centrifugal forces had tended to push apart western and east–central European diplomacy. Another effect of the Armed Neutrality was once more to remind the statesmen of Europe's capitals that Russia had undoubtedly joined the ranks of the great powers. That reminder would be even more firmly conveyed to their successors, the generation of Napoleon I.

12
Conclusion

The character of international relations in Europe underwent profound change during the eighteenth century. Although the language of diplomacy continued to suggest a preoccupation with the succession claims of hereditary ruling families, the underlying reality was different even before Louis XIV's death. The English Revolution of 1689 was a challenge to dynasticism throughout western Europe, a proclamation by the English political nation of its sovereign rights at the expense of the family law of princes. A decade later the partition treaties of 1698 and 1700, though still based on dynastic claims, inaugurated the principle of collective security. The second treaty in particular demonstrates the importance already being attached by the great powers to the idea of state security. By the same token, however, there was no recognition of national identity; indeed, the security needs of the great powers made them entirely indifferent to the wishes of small states like Lorraine, Milan and Ireland. Yet by their very actions these powerful, status-conscious states were beginning to move in a direction which would lead eventually to a world of nation states.

Meanwhile, after the Peace of Utrecht, the principle of collective security guaranteed first the British and French successions and then the cessation of hostilities between the Emperor and Spain. The same principle lay behind the Emperor's efforts to persuade the international community to guarantee the Pragmatic Sanction. By then, however, the key alliance – between Britain and France – had weakened and would shortly be replaced by fierce Franco-British rivalry in Europe and overseas. At the same time a formidable new bloc was emerging in east–central Europe, composed of Austria, Prussia and Russia. By the 1730s, therefore, the old basis of collective security, which had been widely acknowledged after Utrecht, no longer existed, though the wily Cardinal Fleury was still able to exploit the changing situation to neutralise both Lorraine and the Italian peninsula as threats to France's security.

The shift in European power relationships was dramatically demonstrated in 1740 with Frederick the Great's seizure of Silesia and the onset of the War of the Austrian Succession. The issue of security had been prominent in Frederick's calculations yet the effect of his invasion was to destabilise the German world for a generation as Austria and Prussia battled for hegemony. Russia too became an increasingly forceful player in their war games. Ultimately, the partitions of Poland would provide chilling evidence of the evolution of the idea of collective security to a point far beyond the application of traditional legal constraints.

Outside Europe the two Bourbon kingdoms of France and Spain became embroiled in the colonial struggle with Britain, and lost heavily in the process. For both states lacked the resources and the political culture to allow them to maintain an effective challenge to Britain's global commercial strategy. To accompany that strategy a quasi-national sentiment grew up in England. That sentiment, though differently stimulated, also threatened to influence attitudes on the European mainland. For most of the eighteenth century, however, this potentially explosive element was contained within the emerging concept of the impersonal state as the ultimate object of loyalty for all the subjects, and also for the ruler. That powerful idea in turn gave a further boost to the notion of reason of state, by which governments justified policies and actions which contributed to the security and well-being of the state but which could not be justified by any code of personal morality.

Towards the end of the eighteenth century two series of events occurred which finally liberated the genie of nationalism. First came the reforms initiated by Emperor Joseph II which attempted, in the spirit of cameralism, to regulate the affairs of his multi-racial Habsburg inheritance according to a common set of rules. The effect was to make Joseph's subjects increasingly aware of their ethnic, linguistic, cultural and historical distinctiveness as Germans, Czechs, Croats, Serbs, Slovaks, Hungarians, Rumanians, Italians and Netherlanders. Second came the French Revolution. The chief result of that political cataclysm was the birth of the nation state, heir both to the strengthening eighteenth-century tradition of unrestrained state power and to a new aggressive, messianic ideology. Henceforward all the citizens would be so tightly bound in loyalty to their nation that treason would become the most heinous of crimes and the quest for national identity and recognition the supreme objective of policy. Europe had embarked upon a new and dangerously confrontational era of international relations, one from which it has not yet escaped.

Notes

1 'The Origins of the War of the Spanish Succession', in *The Origins of War in Early Modern Europe*, ed. Jeremy Black (Edinburgh: John Donald, 1987), p. 170.
2 'Self-determination and Collective Security as Factors in English and French Foreign Policy, 1689–1718', in *William III and Louis XIV*, ed. R. Hatton and J.S. Bromley (Liverpool: Liverpool University Press, 1968), p. 283.
3 Quoted in B.H. Sumner, *Survey of Russian History* (London: Duckworth, 1944), p. 267.
4 Jeremy Black, *Natural and Necessary Enemies: Anglo-French Relations in the Eighteenth Century* (London: Duckworth, 1986), p. 210.
5 Quoted in Rohan Butler, *Choiseul*, vol. 1 (Oxford: Clarendon Press, 1980), p. 145.
6 Quoted in Leonard Krieger, *An Essay on the Theory of Enlightened Despotism* (Chicago: Chicago University Press, 1975), p. 40.

Further reading

Among contemporary historians Jeremy Black has made the greatest impact in this general field. His works include *Natural and Necessary Enemies: Anglo-French Relations in the Eighteenth Century* (London: Duckworth, 1986); *The Rise of the European Powers, 1679–1793* (London: Edward Arnold, 1990); and *A Military Revolution? Military Change and European Society, 1550–1800* (London: Macmillan, 1991). In addition he has edited and contributed to a volume on *The Origins of War in Early Modern Europe* (Edinburgh: John Donald, 1987). Other recent standard surveys include D. McKay and H.M. Scott, *The Rise of the Great Powers, 1648–1815* (London: Longman, 1983), and M.S. Anderson, *War and Society in Europe of the Old Regime* (London: Fontana, 1988).

Critical moments in the history of European diplomacy are examined in R. Hatton and J.S. Bromley (eds), *William III and Louis XIV* (Liverpool: Liverpool University Press, 1968); D.B. Horn, 'The Diplomatic Revolution', in *New Cambridge Modern History*, vol. 7 (Cambridge: Cambridge University Press, 1957); H. Butterfield, 'The Reconstruction of an Historical Episode: the History of the Enquiry into the Origins of the Seven Years' War', in *Man and his Past* (Cambridge: Cambridge University Press, 1955); T.R. Clayton, 'The Duke of Newcastle, the Earl of Halifax, and the American Origins of the Seven Years' War', *Historical Journal*, 24(3), 1981; Z.E. Rashed, *The Peace of Paris, 1763* (Liverpool: Liverpool University Press, 1951); H.H. Kaplan, *The First Partition of Poland* (New York and London: Columbia University Press, 1962); and Isabel de Madariaga, *Britain, Russia and the Armed Neutrality of 1780* (London: Hollis and Carter, 1962).

In terms of regional coverage see, for Britain, Jeremy Black, *British Foreign Policy in the Age of Walpole* (Edinburgh: John Donald, 1985),

Linda Colley, *Britons: Forging the Nation, 1707–1837* (New Haven and London: Yale University Press, 1992) and U. Dann, *Hanover and Great Britain, 1740–1760* (Leicester: Leicester University Press, 1991); for France, Rohan Butler, *Choiseul*, vol. 1 (Oxford: Clarendon Press, 1980), J.H. Shennan, *Philippe, Duke of Orléans* (London: Thames and Hudson, 1979) and A.M. Wilson, *French Foreign Policy during the Administration of Cardinal Fleury, 1726–1743* (Cambridge, Mass.: Harvard University Press, 1936); for Germany, Michael Hughes, *Early Modern Germany, 1477–1806* (London: Macmillan, 1992) and R. Vierhaus, *Germany in the Age of Absolutism* (trans. J.B. Knudsen, Cambridge: Cambridge University Press, 1988); and for Russia, M.S. Anderson, *Peter the Great* (London: Thames and Hudson, 1978) and Isabel de Madariaga, *Russia in the Age of Catherine the Great* (London: Weidenfeld and Nicolson, 1981).

Finally, the importance of the ideas of cameralism and the Enlightenment are explored in Leonard Krieger, *An Essay on the Theory of Enlightened Despotism* (Chicago: Chicago University Press, 1975) and H.M. Scott (ed.), *Enlightened Absolutism* (London: Macmillan, 1990).